Country Baking

TIME-LIFE BOOKS

Alexandria, Virginia

Country Baking

delicious pies, cakes, cookies, breads, and more for all occasions

A REBUS BOOK

C O N T E N T S

Quick Breads, Coffee Cakes, and Muffins

*simple but rewarding treats for breakfasts, snacks, and
teatime • easy-to-bake loaves in a variety of flavors • sweet and savory
muffins for any time of day • rich fruit- and nut-topped coffee
cakes • sweet raised-dough pastries • features on muffin pans,
gas stoves, and making shaped pastries*

108

Breads, Biscuits, and Crackers

*the staff of life in all its satisfying variety • hearty whole-
grain breads • cheese-laced and herb-flavored loaves and rolls • amusing
flowerpot breads • country-fresh biscuits in a range of regional styles • crunchy
homemade crackers • features on Alaskan sourdough, elegant
dinner rolls, and an impressive ring-shaped bread*

140

CREDITS

170

INDEX

171

ACKNOWLEDGMENTS

175

Pies

*the fruits of fields
and orchards enclosed
in golden crusts*

If one particular food could be said to epitomize American baking, it would surely be pie; in fact, more pie is eaten in this country than in any other. Over the years, the typically American double-crusted pie has come to symbolize all that is wholesome and generous in down-home cooking. Bursting with the fruits of our orchards and fields, freshly baked pies bespeak the bounty of the land and the comforts of the country kitchen.

It is said that New Englanders once ate pie three times a day. But while few New Englanders—or anyone else—would now serve pie at every meal, it is still a favorite dessert for occasions both great and small. "Who can dream of a Thanksgiving dinner without a pie!" wrote Fannie Merritt Farmer in 1896, and her words still ring true today. In this chapter, you will find not only traditional recipes for pies made with apples, blueberries, cranberries, and sweet potatoes, but also some new classics such as peanut butter cup pie and coconut cream pie with a chocolate-coconut crust, both perfectly suited for today's country table.

A hint of orange enlivens a homey Blueberry Pie with Marmalade.

Pastry-Wrapped Pears

Frugal cooks have always saved pastry scraps (left after trimming a pie crust) to concoct homey treats like jam tarts and diminutive dumplings and turnovers. This elegant dessert, suitable for a holiday dinner or other festive meal, expands on the same theme. The pasty-wrapping technique could also be used with apples.

PASTRY
2½ cups flour
2 tablespoons sugar
1 teaspoon salt
1 stick (4 ounces) chilled butter, cut into pieces
5 tablespoons chilled vegetable
   shortening, cut into pieces
8 tablespoons ice water

FILLING AND GLAZE
⅓ cup chopped walnuts
¼ cup apricot preserves
½ teaspoon cinnamon
4 Bosc pears
1 egg yolk
1 tablespoon milk

1. Make the pastry: In a large bowl, combine the flour, sugar, and salt. With a pastry blender or two knives, cut in the butter and shortening until the mixture resembles coarse crumbs.

2. Sprinkle 4 tablespoons of the ice water over the mixture and toss it with a fork. The dough should be just barely moistened, enough so it will hold together when it is formed into a ball. If necessary, add up to 4 tablespoons more water, 1 tablespoon at a time. Divide the dough into 4 pieces, wrap each piece in plastic wrap, and refrigerate for at least 30 minutes.

3. On a lightly floured surface, roll out each piece of dough to a 12 x 10-inch rectangle. From each rectangle, cut a 10 x 10 x 10-inch triangle. Place the triangles on sheets of waxed paper. Cut 16 leaf shapes from the scraps, place them on waxed paper, and use a knife to mark veins on them. Cover the pastry triangles and leaves with plastic wrap and refrigerator them for at least 15 minutes before baking.

4. Meanwhile, make the filling: In a small bowl, stir together the walnuts, preserves, and cinnamon.

5. Without removing the stems, peel the pears. Carefully core each pear from the bottom to within ¾ inch of the stem end, then fill the cavities with the walnut mixture.

6. Line a baking sheet with baking parchment or foil. Lay the pastry triangles on the work surface. Moisten the edges of one triangle with water, then stand a pear in the center of the triangle. Bring the edges of the pastry together to enclose the pear, leaving the stem exposed, and pinch the edges together. Brush the backs of the pastry leaves with water and press them around the tops of the pastry-wrapped pears. Place the pears in the refrigerator for at least 15 minutes before baking.

7. Preheat the oven to 375°.

8. In a small bowl, stir together the egg yolk and milk. Brush the pastry with the egg glaze and bake for 20 to 25 minutes, or until the pastry is lightly browned. Serve the pastry-wrapped pears warm.

Makes 4 pastries

Pastry-Wrapped Pears

Fudge Pie with Gingersnap Crust

Fudge Pie with Gingersnap Crust

Chocolate curls add an elegant finishing touch to this pie. To make the curls, shave the flat side of a chocolate bar with a vegetable peeler, using long, even strokes. For best results, warm the chocolate bar in your hand for a minute or two.

GINGERSNAP CRUST
Thirty-five 2-inch gingersnaps (about 9 ounces)
1 stick (4 ounces) butter, melted
2 tablespoons sugar

FILLING
6 ounces unsweetened chocolate

1 stick (4 ounces) butter
4 eggs
¾ cup (packed) brown sugar
⅔ cup heavy cream
1 teaspoon vanilla extract
Lightly sweetened whipped cream and
  chocolate curls, for garnish (optional)

1. Preheat the oven to 325°.

2. Make the crust: Place the gingersnaps in a food processor or blender and process to form fine crumbs. Turn the crumbs into a bowl, add the melted butter and the sugar, and blend well. Press the crumb mixture evenly into a 9-inch pie plate to form a crust; set aside.

3. Make the filling: In a small heavy saucepan, melt the chocolate and butter, and cook over low heat, stirring until smooth. Remove the pan from the heat and set aside to cool.

4. In a large bowl, beat the eggs. Beat in the sugar, then beat in the cooled chocolate mixture. Beat in the ⅔ cup of heavy cream and the vanilla. Pour the filling into the crust and bake for 25 to 30 minutes, or until the filling is just set. The center may still be slightly wobbly.

5. Let the pie cool to room temperature, then slice it into wedges and top each serving with whipped cream and chocolate curls, if desired.   *Makes one 9-inch pie*

Peanut Butter Cup Pie

For the sweet-toothed, peanut butter (your choice of creamy or chunky) and chocolate should prove an irresistible combination. Invented around the turn of the century, peanut butter was popularized at the 1904 St. Louis World's Fair, which reputedly witnessed the debut of two other American food favorites: the hamburger and the ice cream cone.

Gingersnap Crust (see Fudge Pie, opposite)
3 ounces semisweet chocolate
1 tablespoon butter
1½ cups peanut butter

⅓ cup (packed) brown sugar
1 cup milk
½ cup light cream or half-and-half
1 teaspoon vanilla extract

1. Follow Step 2 of the Fudge Pie recipe to make the Gingersnap Crust.

2. In a small heavy saucepan, melt the chocolate and butter over low heat, stirring until smooth. Remove the pan from the heat and set aside to cool.

3. Make the filling: In a medium bowl, beat the peanut butter until softened and smooth. Gradually beat in the sugar. Add the milk, cream, and vanilla, and continue beating until smooth.

4. Pour the peanut-butter filling into the crust. Pour in the melted chocolate mixture, and gently swirl it through the peanut-butter filling; do not blend completely.

5. Cover the pie with plastic wrap and place in the freezer for at least 6 hours, or overnight.

6. Let the pie stand at room temperature for 15 minutes before serving.

Makes one 9-inch pie

G inger has been a popular ingredient in American baking since colonial times; in fact, ginger cookies were even used to buy votes in 18th-century Virginia. Most current American cookbooks include soft and hard gingerbreads. Earlier sources reveal recipes for sponge gingerbread; for Muster-day gingerbread, which was served to the local militia on training days; for common, fruit, seed, sugar, and even "polka" gingerbreads; and for ginger crisps, ginger nuts, and, of course, gingersnaps.

Glass Rolling Pins

Colorful blown-glass rolling pins were first made in England in the late 18th century. Perhaps because the major glass-makers were located in or near seaports, sailors often bought these decorative rolling pins as souvenirs for their mothers, wives, and sweethearts. Nautical designs or sentimental inscriptions, such as "Be true to me," sometimes adorned these love tokens.

The most renowned producer of glass rolling pins was the Nailsea Glass Works near Bristol, in operation between 1788 and 1873. The word "Nailsea" became synonymous with the style of patterned glass this factory originated, even when the glass was produced far from Bristol, in places such as Yorkshire and Shropshire. The characteristic Nailsea patterns were created by rolling molten glass in colored or white enamel chips. When the glass was reheated and blown into its final shape, the chips became part of the surface design. The ribbony effects, typical of Venetian glass, were probably created by Venetian craftsmen employed by the English factories.

Although intended as souvenirs, the rolling pins could, of course, be used in the kitchen. Some models had corked openings at the ends, which allowed them to be packed with flour for added weight, or to be filled with cracked ice or cold water for rolling pastry in warm weather.

Particularly favored by collectors are patterned glass rolling pins known as "Nailsea;" less flashy etched and plain glass examples are also highly prized.

Cranberry-Pecan Pie with Cornmeal Crust

Instead of pumpkin or mince pie, offer this colorful dessert at Thanksgiving or Christmas dinner, and top it off with a scoop of vanilla ice cream. The refreshingly tart filling, made by combining cranberries with fresh apples, dried apricots, pecans, and maple syrup, tastes like a crunchy cranberry relish. In fact, if the flour is omitted, the fruit and nut mixture can be served as a condiment with poultry or ham.

PASTRY

1 cup flour

⅓ cup yellow cornmeal

2 tablespoons sugar

¾ teaspoon salt

4 tablespoons chilled butter, cut into pieces

3 tablespoons chilled vegetable shortening, cut into pieces

4 to 5 tablespoons ice water

FILLING AND GLAZE

3 cups cranberries

2 medium Granny Smith or other tart green apples, unpeeled and finely chopped

¾ cup dried apricots, chopped

¾ cup chopped pecans

⅓ cup maple syrup

¼ cup flour

1 egg yolk beaten with 1 tablespoon milk

⅓ cup orange marmalade

1. Make the pastry: In a large bowl, combine the flour, cornmeal, sugar, and salt. With a pastry blender or two knives, cut in the butter and shortening until the mixture resembles coarse crumbs.

2. Sprinkle 2 tablespoons of the ice water over the mixture and toss it with a fork. The dough should be just barely moistened, enough so it will hold together when it is formed into a ball. If necessary, add up to 3 tablespoons more water, 1 tablespoon at a time. Form the dough into a flat disk, wrap in plastic wrap, and refrigerate for at least 30 minutes.

3. On a lightly floured surface, roll the dough out to a 12-inch circle. Fit the dough into a 9-inch glass pie plate. Trim the overhang to an even ½ inch and fold it under; crimp the dough to form a decorative border. Prick the pastry with a fork. Place the pie shell in the freezer to chill for at least 15 minutes before baking.

4. Preheat the oven to 400°.

5. Make the filling: In a food processor, pulsing the machine on and off, coarsely chop the cranberries. Transfer the cranberries to a large bowl, add the apples, apricots, pecans, maple syrup, and flour, and stir until well blended; set aside.

6. Line the pie shell with foil and fill it with pie weights or dried beans. Brush the pie border with the egg-yolk mixture and bake for 10 minutes. Remove the pie shell from the oven and reduce the oven temperature to 375°.

7. Remove the foil and weights from the pie shell and spoon the filling into the shell, spreading it evenly with a spatula. Return the pie to the oven and bake it for another 20 minutes, or until the crust is golden; set aside to cool slightly.

8. In a small saucepan, warm the marmalade over low heat until it is pourable. Spoon the warmed marmalade over the cranberry filling. *Makes one 9-inch pie*

Today, fresh whole cranberries are widely available in the fall. They can be put directly into the freezer until needed, or bought already frozen. In 1909, however, a household manual recommended that cooks take them "to a cool upstairs place and stir lightly with the hand occasionally, till dry; then leave them to freeze, as it happens, and they will keep both color and flavor as long as they last."

Cranberry-Pecan Pie with Cornmeal Crust

Oatmeal Breakfast Pie

Pie once was (and in some parts of the country, still is) eaten as part of a hearty American farm breakfast; this homey pie, made with oats, brown rice, and whole-wheat flour, is a wholesome choice for the first meal of the day. Accompany it with some sliced fruit—peaches would be good—and a little cream. Although the pie tastes best on the day it is baked, few cooks keep farmers' hours and would probably prefer to make the pie the day before. It should be reheated for 20 minutes in a 300° oven.

PASTRY

¾ cup whole-wheat flour
½ cup all-purpose flour
⅓ cup old-fashioned rolled oats
¼ teaspoon baking powder
¼ teaspoon salt
4 tablespoons chilled butter, cut into pieces
3 tablespoons chilled vegetable
   shortening, cut into pieces
4 to 5 tablespoons ice water

FILLING

1½ cups milk
¾ cup cooked brown rice
¼ cup sugar
⅓ cup old-fashioned rolled oats
⅓ cup golden raisins
1 teaspoon vanilla extract
½ teaspoon cinnamon
2 eggs

1. Make the pastry: In a large bowl, combine the flours, rolled oats, baking powder, and salt. With a pastry blender or two knives, cut in the butter and shortening until the mixture resembles coarse crumbs.

2. Sprinkle 2 tablespoons of the ice water over the mixture and toss it with a fork. The dough should be just barely moistened, enough so it will hold together when it is formed into a ball. If necessary, add up to 3 tablespoons more water, 1 tablespoon at a time. Form the dough into a flat disk, wrap in plastic wrap, and refrigerate for at least 30 minutes.

3. On a lightly floured surface, roll the dough out to a 12-inch circle. Fit the dough into a 9-inch glass pie plate. Trim the overhang to an even ½ inch all the way around. Fold the overhang under and crimp the dough to form a decorative border. Prick the pastry with a fork. Place the pie shell in the freezer to chill for at least 15 minutes before baking.

4. Preheat the oven to 400°.

5. Line the pie shell with foil, fill it with pie weights or dried beans, and bake it for 10 minutes. Remove the foil and weights, and set the pie shell aside to cool; reduce the oven temperature to 350°.

6. Make the filling: In a medium saucepan, combine the milk, rice, sugar, rolled oats, raisins, vanilla, and cinnamon, and cook over medium heat just until the mixture thickens and bubbles. Remove the pan from the heat.

7. In a small bowl, lightly beat the eggs. Stir ½ cup of the hot milk mixture into the eggs, then pour the egg mixture back into the milk mixture and stir until well blended. Pour the filling into the pie shell and bake it for 20 minutes, or until the filling is set and dry at the edges. Serve the pie warm. *Makes one 9-inch pie*

MAKE-DO PIES

Americans have always hated to give up dessert—especially pie. In times past, when supermarkets did not exist and fruit was only available locally and in season, creative American cooks devised simple substitutes for ingredients they lacked. Their ingenuity resulted in mock apple, mock cherry, mock pecan, and other make-do fillings for pies.

Most Americans are familiar with mock apple pie from the recipe that first graced the back panel of Ritz cracker boxes in the 1940s, and which continued to appear for years thereafter. However, cracker-based mock apple pies have a much longer history in American baking. Enterprising 19th-century cooks contrived a tasty substitute for apples when supplies of the fresh (and dried) fruit ran out. They filled a pastry crust with soda crackers moistened with lemon juice (or vinegar) and a bit of butter, then seasoned them with cinnamon, nutmeg, and other traditional apple pie spices. The crackers plumped up and softened in the baking, and the filling tasted satisfyingly (if surprisingly) like cooked apples.

Over the years ingenious American bakers have created ersatz fillings to approximate the flavors and textures of other favorite pies. For example, a meatless mock mincemeat pie was made by adding rai-

sins, molasses, and cloves to the ever useful soda crackers soaked in vinegar; some variations on the theme used potatoes or green tomatoes in place of crackers.

A mock cherry pie relied on a combination of cranberries and raisins to masquerade as cherries. If fresh lemons were unavailable, a custardy vinegar pie made a convincing substitute for lemon pie. For mock pecan pie, inexpensive dried pinto beans were cooked, chopped, and combined with corn syrup, vanilla, and butter. And for a finishing touch, when there was no cream in the house, some cooks topped their pies, mock or otherwise, with mock whipped cream: beaten egg whites mixed with confectioners' sugar, grated apples, and vanilla.

To make an old-fashioned soda-cracker mock apple pie, use a double-crust 9-inch pie dough recipe. Roll out the bottom crust and line a pie plate with it. Chill for about 30 minutes, or until firm. Meanwhile, make the filling: Crumble 42 unsalted saltines (a 4-ounce package) into a large bowl; stir in 1 cup chopped walnuts and ½ cup raisins; set aside. In a small pan, combine ¼ cup brown sugar, 1 cup apple juice, 2 tablespoons lemon juice, 1 teaspoon grated lemon zest, and ½ teaspoon cinnamon, and bring to a boil. Boil until the sugar has dissolved and the liquid is clear, 2 to 3 minutes. Remove the pan from the heat, let the mixture cool slightly, then add to the crushed cracker mixture. Turn the filling into the pie shell and dot with 1 tablespoon of butter. Roll out the top crust and lay it over the filling. Trim the overhang to an even ½ inch all the way around. Fold the overhang under and crimp the dough to form a decorative border. Cut several steam vents in the top crust, brush with an egg glaze (1 egg yolk beaten with 1 teaspoon water), and sprinkle with 1 teaspoon granulated sugar. Bake the pie at 400° for 20 minutes, or until the crust is golden.

Marlborough Pie

This winter dessert, also known as apple cream pie, is probably of New England origin. Some recipes call for chopped apples, but most use applesauce, which could be made in the fall and canned, or cooked up as needed from dried apples or from fruit wintered-over in a root cellar. In a pinch, substitute 1½ cups of store-bought chunky applesauce, but omit the sugar and Steps 4 and 5. Stir the lemon juice and cinnamon into the applesauce before proceeding with Step 6.

Pie Pastry (recipe follows)
2 medium Granny Smith or other tart
   green apples, peeled and cut into
   coarse chunks (about 3 cups)
½ cup sugar

2 tablespoons lemon juice
½ teaspoon cinnamon
3 eggs
¾ cup heavy cream

1. Make the Pie Pastry.

2. Preheat the oven to 300°.

3. Line the pie shell with foil, fill it with pie weights or dried beans, and bake it for 15 minutes. Remove the foil and weights, and set the pie shell aside to cool. Increase the oven temperature to 325°.

4. Make the filling: In a medium saucepan, combine the apples, sugar, lemon juice, and cinnamon, and bring to a simmer over medium heat, stirring to dissolve the sugar. Reduce the heat to low and simmer, partially covered, until the apples can be easily mashed against the side of the pan with a spoon, about 15 minutes.

5. Remove the pan from the heat and mash the apples, leaving them slightly chunky. Set aside to cool slightly.

6. In a large bowl, beat the eggs until thick and lemon-colored. Add the cooled applesauce and cream, and mix thoroughly.

7. Pour the filling into the pie shell and bake for 30 minutes, or until a knife inserted into the center comes out clean. Serve the pie warm or at room temperature.

Makes one 9-inch pie

Pie Pastry

Marion Harland's "cardinal motto for pastry-makers" in her 1871 book, *Common Sense in the Household*, was "Keep cool . . . . It is harder to make good pastry in warm weather than cold, on account of the tendency of the butter to oil, and thus render the crust heavy and solid." This advice still holds, although it is certainly easier to follow today with the help of refrigeration and air-conditioning.

1¼ cups flour
¾ teaspoon salt
4 tablespoons chilled butter, cut into pieces

3 tablespoons chilled vegetable shortening,
   cut into pieces
4 to 5 tablespoons ice water

1. In a large bowl, combine the flour and salt. With a pastry blender or two knives, cut in the butter and shortening until the mixture resembles coarse crumbs.

2. Sprinkle 2 tablespoons of the ice water over the mixture and toss it with a fork. The dough should be just barely moistened, enough so it will hold together when it is formed into a ball. If necessary, add up to 3 tablespoons more water, 1 tablespoon at a time. Form the dough into a flat disk, wrap in plastic wrap, and refrigerate for at least 30 minutes.

3. On a lightly floured surface, roll the dough out to a 12-inch circle. Fit the dough into a 9-inch glass pie plate. Trim the overhang to an even ½ inch all the way around. Fold the overhang under and crimp the dough to form a decorative border. Prick the pastry with a fork. Place the pie shell in the freezer to chill for at least 15 minutes before baking. *Makes one 9-inch crust*

Shoofly Pie

To make this warmly spiced Pennsylvania-German specialty, you first prepare a rich butter crumble: part of it will be used in the filling, while the remainder will be needed for the crusty topping. This variation, with its moist filling, is referred to as a "wet" shoofly pie; so-called "dry" versions have a more cakelike texture, and are suitable for dunking. Both types demand strong, hot coffee as an accompaniment.

Pie Pastry (opposite)	3 tablespoons chilled butter, cut into pieces
1 cup flour	1 egg
½ cup to 1 cup (packed) brown sugar	¾ cup light unsulphured molasses
½ teaspoon cinnamon	1 cup boiling water
½ teaspoon nutmeg	1 teaspoon baking soda

1. Make the Pie Pastry.

2. Preheat the oven to 450°.

3. In a large bowl, combine the flour, sugar, cinnamon, and nutmeg. With a pastry blender or two knives, cut in the butter until the mixture resembles coarse crumbs. (Don't worry if the dry ingredients do not appear to be completely incorporated at this stage.)

4. In a medium bowl, lightly beat the egg. Beat in the molasses; set aside.

5. Pour the boiling water into a heatproof cup and stir in the baking soda. Gradually add the baking soda mixture to the molasses mixture, beating until well incorporated.

6. Remove the pie shell from the freezer. Stir 1 cup of the crumb mixture into the molasses mixture, and pour it into the pie shell. Sprinkle the remaining crumb mixture evenly over the filling and place the pie in the oven. Reduce the oven temperature to 350° and bake the pie for about 30 minutes, or until the filling is set and puffed, and does not quiver when the pie is shaken gently. Serve the pie slightly warm or at room temperature. *Makes one 9-inch pie*

Jefferson Davis Pie

Some recipes for Jefferson Davis pie contain a variety of spices. This version is flavored simply with vanilla and nutmeg; the taste is reminiscent of eggnog.

Pie Pastry (page 20)
¾ cup sugar
1 stick (4 ounces) butter, softened to
   room temperature
3 eggs

1 cup heavy cream
½ cup milk
2 tablespoons flour
1 teaspoon vanilla extract
½ teaspoon nutmeg

1. Make the Pie Pastry.
2. Preheat the oven to 400°.
3. Line the pie shell with foil, fill it with pie weights or dried beans, and bake it for 10 minutes. Remove the foil and weights, and set the pie shell aside to cool; reduce the oven temperature to 375°.
4. Make the filling: In a large bowl, cream the sugar and butter. Gradually beat in the eggs, cream, milk, flour, vanilla, and nutmeg. Pour the filling into the pie shell and bake for 20 minutes.
5. Reduce the oven temperature to 300° and bake for another 10 minutes, or until the filling is set and golden. Serve the pie warm or at room temperature.

Makes one 9-inch pie

*S*cornful Yankees applied the name of Jefferson Davis, president of the Confederacy, to some Southern make-do foods necessitated by wartime shortages. For instance, "Jeff Davis coffee" was brewed from roasted grain. However, the origin of Jefferson Davis Pie has been traced to a cook whose master greatly admired the leader of the seceded states.

Raisin·Currant Pie

Dried currants distinguish this attractive variation on the classic Pennsylvania-German raisin pie, a year-round favorite. If currants are not available, however, dark raisins would make an excellent substitute.

PASTRY
1¼ cups flour
¾ teaspoon salt
4 tablespoons chilled butter, cut into
   pieces
3 tablespoons chilled vegetable
   shortening, cut into pieces
¼ cup sour cream
1 to 2 tablespoons ice water
1 egg yolk beaten with 1 tablespoon milk

FILLING
2½ cups water
¼ cup flour
2 cups dried currants
1¼ cups golden raisins
¼ cup (packed) brown sugar
3 tablespoons lemon juice
1 tablespoon brandy
1 tablespoon butter
1 teaspoon grated lemon zest

1. Make the pastry: In a large bowl, combine the flour and salt. With a pastry blender or two knives, cut in the butter and shortening until the mixture resembles coarse crumbs. Add the sour cream and 1 tablespoon of the ice water, and toss the mixture with a fork. The dough should be just barely moistened, enough so it will hold

Raisin-Currant Pie

together when it is formed into a ball. If necessary, add up to 1 tablespoon more water. Form the dough into a flat disk, wrap in plastic wrap, and refrigerate for at least 30 minutes.

2. On a lightly floured surface, roll the dough out to a 12-inch circle. Fit the dough into a 9-inch glass pie plate. Trim the overhang to an even ½ inch all the way around. Fold the overhang under and crimp it to form a border. Prick the pastry with a fork. Place the pie shell in the freezer to chill for at least 15 minutes before baking.

3. Preheat the oven to 400°.

4. Line the pie shell with foil and fill it with pie weights or dried beans. Brush the pie border with the egg-yolk mixture and bake for 15 minutes. Remove the foil and weights, and set the pie shell aside to cool; reduce the oven temperature to 300°.

5. Make the filling: In a small bowl, stir together ¼ cup of the water and the flour; set aside. In a medium saucepan, combine the currants, raisins, and the remaining 2¼ cups water. Cook over medium heat, stirring often, until the mixture comes to a boil. Remove from the heat, add the flour mixture and sugar, and stir until well blended. Return the pan to the heat and cook, stirring often, until the mixture returns to a boil. Boil the mixture until it is slightly thickened, 1 to 2 minutes. Remove from the heat and blend in the lemon juice, brandy, butter, and lemon zest.

6. Pour the filling into the pie shell and spread it evenly with a spatula. Bake the pie for 30 minutes, or until the crust is lightly browned. Serve the pie warm.

Makes one 9-inch pie

DECORATIVE PIE BORDERS

RIDGED FLUTE

A ridged flute is one of the easiest ways to dress up a pie. After trimming the overhang to an even ½ inch all around and turning it under, flute the dough by pinching it with the thumb and forefinger of one hand against the thumb of the other hand. Then, using your hand to support the flutes from underneath, press the tines of a fork into the pastry. This method should also flare the border out slightly without flattening it onto the rim of the pie plate.

AUTUMN LEAVES

Making a border of autumn leaves requires extra dough; see the pastry recipe for Sweet Potato Pie with Almond Topping (page 28) as a guide for quantities. Use two-thirds of the dough to line the pie plate, trim the overhang to an even ½ inch all around, and turn it under. Roll out the remaining dough to a thickness of about ⅛ inch and, with a knife, cut out leaf shapes of varying sizes. If desired, score vein patterns in the leaves with the tip of the knife. Pour the filling into the pie shell and then use egg yolk to attach the leaves to the edge of the pie. Let some of the leaves extend inward, beyond the pie edge and over the filling.

BRAIDED BORDER

A braided border adds a homey touch to any pie. Use a double-crust pastry recipe: half to line the pie plate and half for the braids. To make the braids, halve the reserved dough and roll out each half to a 20 x 1½-inch strip. Then, cut each strip into three smaller ½-inch-wide strips. Leaving the strips on the work surface, carefully braid each set. Brush the edge of the pie with egg glaze. Gently transfer the two braids to the pie and lightly press to secure them.

CASTLE TOP

Here is a marvelously simple but impressive treatment for a pie border. The castle top is suitable for a pie with a prebaked shell and an uncooked filling as well as for a pie whose filling and crust are baked together—the filling can help to support the border as it bakes. To make the border, use a single-crust pastry recipe to line the pie plate. Trim the overhang to an even ½ inch all around and turn it under; press lightly to seal and form a thick border. With a pair of kitchen scissors or a sharp knife, make cuts the full depth of the border, spaced about ¾ inch apart. Then fold in every other section of dough toward the center.

Sweet-Potato Pie with Almond Topping

Sweet potatoes are a Southern staple, and although pumpkin pies are also served in the South, sweet-potato-based desserts are more characteristic of the region. A rich, mellow flavor makes this pie a perfect conclusion to Thanksgiving dinner.

PASTRY
1¼ cups flour
½ cup yellow cornmeal
1 tablespoon granulated sugar
¾ teaspoon salt
6 tablespoons chilled butter, cut into pieces
4 tablespoons chilled vegetable
   shortening, cut into pieces
5 to 8 tablespoons ice water

FILLING
4 tablespoons butter, softened to room
   temperature
½ cup (packed) light brown sugar

2 large sweet potatoes, baked, peeled, and
   smoothly mashed (about 2 cups)
2 eggs, lightly beaten
½ cup heavy cream
1 tablespoon grated orange zest
½ teaspoon cinnamon

TOPPING AND GLAZE
¼ cup sliced almonds
1½ tablespoons flour
1½ tablespoons (packed) dark brown sugar
1 tablespoon chilled butter
1 egg yolk
1 tablespoon milk

1. Make the pastry: In a large bowl, combine the flour, cornmeal, granulated sugar, and salt. With a pastry blender or two knives, cut in the butter and shortening until the mixture resembles coarse crumbs.

2. Sprinkle 2 tablespoons of the ice water over the mixture and toss it with a fork. The dough should be just barely moistened, enough so it will hold together when it is formed into a ball. If necessary, add up to 6 tablespoons more water, 1 tablespoon at a time. Form the dough into a flat disk, wrap in plastic wrap, and refrigerate for at least 30 minutes. (If desired, use one-third of the dough to make a leaf border—see Decorative Pie Borders, pages 26-27.)

3. On a lightly floured surface, roll out the dough to a 12-inch circle. Fit the dough into a 9-inch glass pie plate. Trim the overhang to an even ½ inch all the way around. Fold the overhang under. Prick the bottom and sides of the pastry with a fork. Place the pie shell in the freezer to chill for at least 15 minutes before baking.

4. Make the filling: In a large bowl, cream the butter and light brown sugar until light and fluffy. Beat in the sweet potato until it is completely incorporated, then beat in the eggs. Add the cream, orange zest, and cinnamon, and continue beating until the mixture is smooth; set aside.

5. Preheat the oven to 350°.

6. Make the topping: Spread the almonds on a baking sheet and toast them in the oven, stirring occasionally, until golden, 5 to 10 minutes; set aside to cool briefly.

7. In a small bowl, combine the flour and dark brown sugar. Cut in the butter until the mixture resembles coarse crumbs. Stir in the almonds; set aside.

8. Make the egg glaze: In a small bowl, beat the egg yolk with the milk; set aside.

9. Spread the filling evenly in the pie shell, then sprinkle the topping over the

center of the filling. Brush the border of the crust with the egg glaze (if making the leaf border, use some of the egg-milk glaze to stick the leaves onto the pie border). Bake the pie for 30 to 35 minutes, or until the crust is golden. (If you have made the leaf border and it is browning too quickly, cover it with a crimped piece of foil.)

Makes one 9-inch pie

Osgood Pie

Osgood Pie (the name originally may have been "Oh So Good") belongs to the chess pie family. These pies, including pecan pie and Jefferson Davis Pie (page 22), have butter, eggs, and sugar (or molasses or syrup) as their basic filling ingredients. Stiffly beaten egg whites give Osgood Pie a light, cakelike texture, while nuts, fruit, and sweet spices impart a rich flavor reminiscent of fruitcake.

Pie Pastry (page 20)
1 cup chopped pecans
1 cup dried apricots, chopped
1 cup raisins
1 tablespoon flour
½ teaspoon allspice

½ teaspoon cinnamon
½ teapoon nutmeg
3 eggs, separated
½ cup sugar
2 tablespoons butter, melted
2 tablespoons cider vinegar

1. Make the Pie Pastry.

2. Preheat the oven to 400°.

3. Line the pie shell with foil, fill it with pie weights or dried beans, and bake it for 10 minutes. Remove the foil and weights and set the pie shell aside to cool; reduce the oven temperature to 375°.

4. Make the filling: In a large bowl combine the pecans, apricots, raisins, flour, allspice, cinnamon, and nutmeg, and toss to coat the nuts and fruit with the flour and spices; set aside.

5. Place the egg yolks in a large bowl. Gradually beat in the sugar and continue beating until the mixture is thick and light-colored. Add the butter and vinegar, and stir to blend. Stir in the nut and fruit mixture; set aside.

6. In another large bowl, beat the egg whites until stiff but not dry. Using a rubber spatula, gently fold the beaten whites into the nut and fruit mixture.

7. Spread the mixture evenly in the pie shell and bake for 18 to 20 minutes, or until the filling is set and golden, and a knife inserted into the center of the pie comes out clean. Serve warm.

Makes one 9-inch crust

Grasshopper Pie

Black Bottom Pie

The South takes credit for this recipe, which was a favorite of Floridian Marjorie Kinnan Rawlings, author of *Cross Creek Cookery* (and of *The Yearling*).

CHOCOLATE COOKIE CRUST
1 package (8½ ounces) chocolate wafers
⅓ cup butter, melted

FILLING AND TOPPING
3 ounces unsweetened chocolate
1 teaspoon vanilla extract
3 eggs, separated, plus 1 egg yolk
1 envelope unflavored gelatin

2 cups cold milk
2 tablespoons cornstarch
⅔ cup granulated sugar
¼ teaspoon salt
¼ teaspoon cream of tartar
2 tablespoons dark rum
Sweetened whipped cream and chocolate
*   shavings, for garnish*

1. Make the crust: Place the wafers in a food processor or blender and process to form fine crumbs. Turn the crumbs into a bowl, add the melted butter, and blend well. Press the crumb mixture evenly into a 9-inch pie plate to form a crust; set aside.

2. Make the filling: In the top of a double boiler over hot, not simmering, water, melt the chocolate. Remove the pan from the heat, stir in the vanilla, and set aside.

3. In a small bowl, lightly beat the 4 egg yolks. In another small bowl, sprinkle the gelatin over ¼ cup of the milk. In a third small bowl, stir together the cornstarch and another ¼ cup of the milk. Set aside.

4. In a medium saucepan, scald the remaining 1½ cups milk. Stir ½ cup of the hot milk into the egg yolks; then stir in ⅓ cup of the granulated sugar, the cornstarch mixture, and the salt. Pour the egg-yolk mixture into the pan of hot milk and cook over medium heat, stirring constantly, until the custard is thick enough to coat the back of a spoon, 5 to 8 minutes. Stir in the gelatin mixture.

5. Divide the custard into two parts. Stir the chocolate mixture into one part, then immediately pour it into the crust. Set the remaining custard aside to cool.

6. In a large bowl, beat the egg whites until frothy. Add the cream of tartar and beat until soft peaks form. Gradually add the remaining ⅓ cup granulated sugar and continue beating until stiff peaks form.

7. Fold the beaten whites into the cooled custard, then gently stir in the rum. Spread the mixture carefully over the chocolate layer in the pie crust. Cover the pie with plastic wrap and refrigerate until well chilled and set, 3 to 4 hours.

8. Just before serving, top the pie with whipped cream and chocolate shavings.

Makes one 9-inch pie

Grasshopper Pie

Like the creamy cocktail for which it is named, Grasshopper Pie gets its vivid color from green crème de menthe, a mint-flavored liqueur. If crème de cacao (which is a chocolate-flavored liqueur) is not available, add a quarter-cup more crème de menthe.

*Chocolate Cookie Crust (see Black Bottom
   Pie, opposite)*
1 cup light cream or half-and-half
36 large marshmallows (4½ cups)
¼ cup green crème de menthe

¼ cup crème de cacao
2½ cups heavy cream
2 tablespoons confectioners' sugar
Chocolate shavings, for garnish (optional)

1. Follow Step 1 of the Black Bottom Pie recipe to make the Chocolate Cookie Crust; set aside.

2. In a medium saucepan, combine the light cream and marshmallows, and cook over medium heat, stirring constantly, until the marshmallows are completely melted, about 5 minutes. Remove the pan from the heat and stir in the crème de menthe and crème de cacao. Cover the pan and set the filling aside to cool to room temperature.

3. When the filling is cool, in a large bowl, beat 1½ cups of the heavy cream until stiff. Stir one-fourth of the whipped cream into the filling. Fold in the remaining whipped cream, then turn the filling into the crust, spreading it evenly with a rubber spatula. Place the pie in the freezer for at least 6 hours, or overnight.

4. Allow the pie to stand at room temperature for 15 minutes before serving.

5. Meanwhile, make the topping: Whip the remaining 1 cup heavy cream with the confectioners' sugar until stiff. Top the pie with the whipped cream and sprinkle with chocolate shavings, if desired.

Makes one 9-inch pie

Although chilled and frozen desserts have existed for centuries, they did not become generally popular until refrigerators were common in middle-class households. The recipe books that came with new refrigerators in the 1930s and '40s included instructions for Black Bottom Pie and for frozen desserts called "marlows," confected of marshmallows, whipped cream, and various flavorings.

Red, White, and Blue Pie

For many people, Independence Day means a picnic, and no picnic is really a picnic without a pie. This glorious dessert makes the best of summer's berries, and carries out the patriotic color scheme as well. To simplify your picnic-day plans, bake the crust the night before, then fill and decorate the pie shortly before serving time.

PASTRY
1¼ cups flour
2 tablespoons granulated sugar
7 tablespoons chilled butter, cut into pieces
4 to 5 tablespoons ice water

FILLING AND TOPPING
5 cups strawberries (2 pints)

2½ cups blueberries (1 pint)
¼ cup lemon juice
3 tablespoons cold water
1 tablespoon arrowroot or cornstarch
¼ cup granulated sugar
½ cup heavy cream
1 tablespoon confectioners' sugar

1. Make the pastry: In a large bowl, combine the flour and granulated sugar. With a pastry blender or two knives, cut in the butter until the mixture resembles coarse crumbs.

2. Sprinkle 2 tablespoons of the ice water over the mixture and toss it with a fork. The dough should be just barely moistened, enough so it will hold together when it is formed into a ball. If necessary, add up to 3 tablespoons more water, 1 tablespoon at a time. Form the dough into a flat disk, wrap in plastic wrap, and refrigerate for at least 30 minutes.

3. On a lightly floured surface, roll the dough out to a 12-inch circle. Fit the dough into a 9-inch glass pie plate. Trim the overhang to an even ½ inch all the way around. Fold the overhang under and crimp the dough to form a decorative border. Prick the pastry with a fork. Place the pie shell in the freezer to chill for at least 15 minutes before baking.

4. Preheat the oven to 400°.

5. Line the pie shell with foil, fill it with pie weights or dried beans, and bake for 10 minutes. Remove the foil and weights, reduce the oven temperature to 375°, and bake for another 10 to 12 minutes, or until light golden. Set aside to cool.

6. Place 1 cup of the strawberries and ½ cup of the blueberries in a small saucepan and crush them with a fork. In a small bowl, stir together the lemon juice, water, and arrowroot until blended, then add this mixture to the crushed berries. Stir in the granulated sugar, and cook over medium heat, stirring constantly, for 5 minutes, or until the mixture thickens and becomes translucent. Cover the berry glaze with plastic wrap and set aside to cool completely.

7. Place the remaining 4 cups strawberries and 2 cups blueberries in a medium bowl, pour the cooled berry glaze over them, and toss gently to coat. Spoon the berry mixture into the pie shell and refrigerate the pie until serving time.

8. Just before serving, make the topping: In a medium bowl, whip the cream with the confectioners' sugar until stiff. Spoon or pipe the sweetened whipped cream decoratively on top of the pie.

Makes one 9-inch pie

Red, White, and Blue Pie

Rustic fruit Pies

Here is an easy way to give a country look to a double-crust pie. Instead of top and bottom crusts, a single large crust is used to enclose the filling in a rustic-looking bundle. This method is well suited to fruit pies, and works best with fruits that hold their shape, such as apples, nectarines, peaches, and plums. The method is comfortably flexible: Precision in rolling out and trimming the crust is not necessary, and the pie need not be baked in a round pie plate. As long as it holds about 1½ quarts, you can use any shape baking dish you like. When using a square-cornered dish, however, you should trim some dough from the folds in the corners; otherwise, they will be too thick and may not fully bake.

A. Roll the dough out to a 15-inch circle. Keep the rolling pin and the work surface lightly floured to avoid sticking.

APPLE PIE WITH CHEDDAR CRUST

PASTRY
2¼ cups flour
½ teaspoon salt
10 tablespoons chilled butter, cut
    into pieces
1 cup grated Cheddar cheese
    (about ¼ pound)
5 to 6 tablespoons ice water

FILLING
3 medium Granny Smith apples,
    unpeeled and cubed (about 3
    cups)

1 tablespoon apple cider vinegar
¾ cup fresh breadcrumbs
⅓ cup (packed) light or dark
    brown sugar
½ cup finely chopped walnuts
¼ cup golden raisins
¼ teaspoon cinnamon
¼ teaspoon nutmeg
1 tablespoon butter

EGG GLAZE
1 egg yolk beaten with 1
    tablespoon milk

1. Make the pastry: In a large bowl, combine the flour and salt. With a pastry blender or two knives, cut in the chilled butter until the mixture resembles coarse crumbs. Stir in the grated cheese. Sprinkle 4 tablespoons of the ice water over the mixture and toss it with a fork. The dough should be just barely moistened, enough so it will hold together when it is formed into a ball. If necessary, add up to 2 tablespoons more water. Form the dough into a disk, wrap in plastic wrap, and refrigerate for at least 30 minutes.

2. Make the filling: Place the apples in a large bowl and sprinkle them with the vinegar. In a medium bowl, combine the breadcrumbs, sugar, walnuts, raisins, cinnamon, and nutmeg, and stir with a fork to mix well. Add the breadcrumb mixture to the apples and toss until they are well combined.

3. Preheat the oven to 425°.

4. On a lightly floured surface, roll the dough out to a 15-inch circle (Illustration A).

5. Line a 1½-quart deep-dish pie plate with the dough, letting the extra dough hang over the edges. Spoon the filling into the pie shell, mounding it slightly in the center (Illustration B). Dot the filling with the butter.

6. Gather up the dough overhang and fold it over the filling, leaving a 3- to 4-inch opening in the center (Illustration C). Brush the pie crust with the glaze and bake for 25 to 30 minutes, or until the crust is golden.

Makes one 9-inch pie

B. Fit the dough into the baking dish, letting the edges hang over evenly all the way around. Spoon in the filling.

C. Bring the edges of the dough up over the filling, leaving an opening in the center. Brush with the egg glaze.

Banana-Strawberry Cream Pie

Banana cream pie is an American classic, but its smooth sweetness can be somewhat boring. Layering some fresh strawberries with the custard, bananas, and whipped cream adds a new spark to this family favorite. The ground toasted almonds in the crust add further variety of texture and flavor.

PASTRY
½ cup slivered blanched almonds
1⅓ cups flour
1 tablespoon granulated sugar
½ teaspoon salt
4 tablespoons chilled butter, cut into pieces
3 tablespoons chilled vegetable
   shortening, cut into pieces
4 to 5 tablespoons ice water

FILLING AND TOPPING
¼ cup flour

⅓ cup granulated sugar
3 egg yolks
1½ cups milk
1 tablespoon butter
1 teaspoon vanilla extract
4 ripe bananas
3 tablespoons lemon juice
2 cups strawberries
1 cup heavy cream
2 tablespoons confectioners' sugar

1. Preheat the oven to 375°.

2. Make the pastry: Spread the almonds in a shallow baking pan and toast them in the oven, stirring occasionally, for 5 minutes, or until golden. Turn off the oven. Transfer the almonds to a food processor and process just until finely ground, about 30 seconds; do not overprocess or the almonds will turn into an oily paste.

3. In a large bowl, combine the ground almonds, flour, granulated sugar, and salt. With a pastry blender or two knives, cut in the butter and shortening until the mixture resembles coarse crumbs.

4. Sprinkle 2 tablespoons of the ice water over the mixture and toss it with a fork. The dough should be just barely moistened, enough so it will hold together when it is formed into a ball. If necessary, add up to 3 tablespoons more water, 1 tablespoon at a time. Form the dough into a flat disk, wrap in plastic wrap, and refrigerate for at least 30 minutes.

5. On a lightly floured surface, roll the dough out to a 12-inch circle. Fit the dough into a 9-inch glass pie plate. Trim the overhang to an even ½ inch all the way around. Fold the overhang under and crimp the dough to form a decorative border. Prick the pastry with a fork. Place the pie shell in the freezer to chill for at least 15 minutes before baking.

6. Preheat the oven to 375°.

7. Line the pie shell with foil, fill it with pie weights or dried beans, and bake it for 10 minutes. Remove the foil and weights, and bake the pie shell for another 7 minutes, or until golden. Remove the pie shell from the oven and set it aside to cool.

8. Make the filling: In a medium saucepan, combine the flour and granulated sugar. Beat in the egg yolks, one at a time, then gradually add the milk, whisking constantly. Place the pan over medium heat. When the mixture has almost come to a

boil, reduce the heat to low and simmer, stirring constantly, until it is thick and custardy. Stir in the butter and vanilla, remove the pan from the heat, and set the filling aside to cool. Place a circle of waxed paper directly on the surface of the custard to prevent a skin from forming.

9. Slice the bananas ¼ inch thick and place them in a bowl. Sprinkle the lemon juice over them and toss to coat. Halve any large strawberries.

10. Spread half of the custard evenly in the pie shell, and arrange a layer of bananas and strawberries on top. Top with the remaining custard, bananas, and strawberries. Refrigerate the pie for at least 1 hour.

11. Before serving, make the topping: In a medium bowl, whip the cream with the confectioners' sugar until stiff. Spoon the whipped cream on top of the pie.

Makes one 9-inch pie

Tyler Pudding Pie

President John Tyler is one of several American political luminaries and military heroes to have had desserts named in their honor: Lafayette Gingerbread and Robert E. Lee Cake are two other examples. Virginia-born Tyler's name was given to this creation, which is buttery and caramel-flavored but not excessively sweet. It is said to have been served often at the White House during the Tyler administration.

Pie Pastry (page 20), made with
7 tablespoons of butter (omit the
vegetable shortening)

FILLING
2 eggs plus 2 egg yolks

1 cup (packed) brown sugar
1 stick (4 ounces) butter
½ cup heavy cream
½ teaspoon vanilla extract
¼ teaspoon nutmeg

1. Make the all-butter Pie Pastry; reserve the scraps.
2. Preheat the oven to 400°.
3. Line the pie shell with foil, fill it with pie weights or dried beans, and bake it for 10 minutes. Meanwhile, roll out the scraps of dough and cut out small stars or other decorative shapes; set aside. Remove the foil and weights from the pie shell and set it aside to cool; reduce the oven temperature to 375°.
4. Make the filling: In a medium bowl, beat the eggs and egg yolks until pale; set aside.
5. In a medium saucepan, combine the sugar, butter, and cream. Cook over medium heat, stirring constantly, until the sugar has dissolved and the butter is melted, 5 to 7 minutes.
6. Remove the pan from the heat and slowly add the beaten eggs, beating constantly. Stir in the vanilla and nutmeg, then pour the filling into the pie shell.
7. Arrange the pastry cutouts on top of the filling and bake for 20 minutes, or until the filling is puffed and rippled. Serve the pie warm. *Makes one 9-inch pie*

FRIED PIES

Known variously as half-moon pies, mule ears, or crab lanterns—because of their semicircular shape—fried pies are usually associated with the South, although there are parts of New England that also lay claim to them.

These diminutive, deep-fried turnovers (small disks of dough folded over a fruit filling) are homey and satisfying. Not only are fried pies delightful for breakfast, afternoon snacks, or dessert, but, like other pastry-wrapped foods, they are eminently portable, making them perfect for lunchboxes, picnics, and other "fingerfood" situations. In fact, such pies were sometimes brought to church to keep restless children quiet, giving rise to yet another name, "preaching pies."

Traditionally, fried pies were filled with dried fruit; dried peaches, in particular, defined the Southern fried pie. Dried apples were also popular, and in New England, fried pies were often filled with applesauce. The use of dried fruits was motivated by practical, as much as gustatory, considerations, since fresh fruit was not available during the winter. A housewife's treasured stock of dried fruit was often the product of peach or apple bees, where women gathered to peel, slice, and dry fruit after the harvest.

Recipes for fried pies vary. Most call for a sturdy pie dough made with less fat than usual; but there are recipes that use biscuit or doughnut dough. The fruit for the filling can be puréed or simply cooked until softened; and the amount of sugar and the kinds of spices used in a fried pie remain at the whim of the cook.

Buttermilk-Lemon Pie

Traditionally, this dessert was made in the winter, when the fresh fruit needed for pie fillings was unavailable. Pantries, however, were always stocked with flour, butter, eggs, milk, and sugar; vinegar could be used if there were no lemons on hand. This pie is unusual in that its thick custard filling, when baked, separates into two layers. The top is firm and rather cakelike; the bottom is soft and custardy.

PASTRY
1¼ cups flour
¾ teaspoon salt
7 tablespoons chilled butter, cut into pieces
3 tablespoons buttermilk
2 to 3 tablespoons ice water

FILLING
1 stick (4 ounces) butter, softened to
   room temperature

¾ cup sugar
3 eggs plus 2 egg yolks
¼ cup flour
1 cup buttermilk
1 tablespoon lemon juice
1 tablespoon grated lemon zest
1 teaspoon vanilla extract
½ teaspoon nutmeg

1. In a large bowl, combine the flour and salt. With a pastry blender or two knives, cut in the butter until the mixture resembles coarse crumbs.

2. Sprinkle the buttermilk and 1 tablespoon of ice water over the mixture and toss it with a fork. The dough should be just barely moistened, enough so it will hold together when it is formed into a ball. If necessary, add up to 2 tablespoons more water, 1 tablespoon at a time. Form the dough into a flat disk, wrap in plastic wrap, and refrigerate for at least 30 minutes.

3. On a lightly floured surface, roll the dough out to a 12-inch circle. Fit the dough into a 9-inch glass pie plate. Trim the overhang to an even ½ inch all the way around. Fold the overhang under and crimp the dough to form a decorative border. Prick the pastry with a fork. Place the pie shell in the freezer to chill for at least 15 minutes before baking.

4. Preheat the oven to 400°.

5. Line the pie shell with foil, fill it with pie weights or dried beans, and bake it for 10 minutes. Remove the foil and weights, and set the pie shell aside to cool; reduce the oven temperature to 350°.

6. Make the filling: In a large bowl, cream the butter and sugar until light and fluffy. Beat in the eggs and yolks one at a time, beating well after each addition. Beat in the flour. Still beating, slowly pour in the buttermilk, then stir in the lemon juice, zest, vanilla, and nutmeg.

7. Pour the filling into the pie shell and bake for 25 to 30 minutes, or until the filling is firm and golden. Cool the pie to room temperature before serving.

Makes one 9-inch pie

Coconut Cream Pie with Chocolate-Coconut Crust

This no-bake pie (except for toasting the coconut) is perfect for hot-weather entertaining, but its delightful flavor justifies serving it through the year. Toasted coconut enhances the pie in a number of ways: Some of it is mixed with melted chocolate to form a crunchy crust; a generous amount is blended into the rich custard filling to give it a nut-like flavor; and the remaining portion is sprinkled over dollops of whipped cream to make an attractive topping.

1 package (7 ounces) sweetened shredded coconut (about 3 cups)
3 ounces semisweet chocolate
2 tablespoons butter
⅓ cup granulated sugar
¼ cup cornstarch

4 egg yolks
2 cups milk
½ teaspoon coconut extract
½ cup heavy cream
2 tablespoons confectioners' sugar

1. Preheat the oven to 325°.

2. Spread the coconut in a large, shallow baking pan and toast it in the oven, stirring occasionally, until lightly browned, about 10 minutes.

3. Meanwhile, in the top of a double boiler over hot, not simmering, water, melt the chocolate and butter. Remove the pan from the heat and stir 2 cups of the toasted coconut into the chocolate mixture.

4. Turn the coconut-chocolate mixture into a 9-inch pie plate and pat it evenly into the plate to form a crust. Cover the crust with plastic wrap and refrigerate it for at least 15 minutes, or until firm.

5. Meanwhile, make the filling: In a medium saucepan, combine the granulated sugar and cornstarch. Gradually whisk in the egg yolks, then slowly add the milk, whisking constantly, until the mixture is smooth and the sugar is dissolved. Place the pan over medium heat, and cook the mixture, whisking constantly, until it is thick enough to coat the back of a spoon, 5 to 10 minutes.

6. Stir in the coconut extract and ¾ cup of the remaining toasted coconut. Let the filling cool slightly, then place a circle of waxed paper directly on the surface of the custard to prevent a skin from forming. Place the filling in the refrigerator to chill for at least one hour.

7. Just before serving, make the whipped cream topping: In a medium bowl, whip the cream with the confectioners' sugar until stiff.

8. Spoon the filling into the crust. Top the pie with the whipped cream, then sprinkle with the remaining ¼ cup coconut. *Makes one 9-inch pie*

Lemon-Orange Meringue Pie

Under its lofty topping, this pie conceals a flavor twist—a hint of orange in the classic lemon filling. A golden meringue-crowned pie is a proud achievement for any baker, and despite its impressive appearance, it isn't really a difficult dessert to prepare. One basic rule to follow: When spooning the meringue over the filling, be sure to spread it evenly to the edges so that the topping touches the crust all the way around. This will help prevent the meringue from shrinking as it bakes.

Pie Pastry (page 20)
¾ cup plus ⅓ cup sugar
¼ cup cornstarch
3 tablespoons flour
1¾ cups milk
4 eggs, separated

⅓ cup lemon juice
2 tablespoons butter, cut into pieces
1 tablespoon grated lemon zest
1 tablespoon grated orange zest
1 teaspoon orange extract
¼ teaspoon cream of tartar

1. Make the Pie Pastry.

2. Preheat the oven to 400°.

3. Line the pie shell with foil, fill it with pie weights or dried beans, and bake it for 10 minutes. Remove the foil and weights, and set the pie shell aside to cool; reduce the oven temperature to 350°.

4. Make the filling: In a medium saucepan, combine ¾ cup of the sugar, the cornstarch, and flour. Place the pan over medium heat and slowly add the milk, whisking constantly. Continue cooking and whisking until the mixture is thick enough to coat the back of a spoon. Remove the pan from the heat and let the mixture cool slightly.

5. Add the egg yolks, one at a time. Then add the lemon juice, and whisk until well blended. One ingredient at a time, add the butter, lemon and orange zests, and orange extract, whisking well after each addition; the custard should be very thick. Set the pan in a large bowl of cold water to cool for about 5 minutes.

6. Meanwhile, make the meringue: In a large bowl, beat the egg whites until frothy. Add the cream of tartar and continue beating until soft peaks form. Gradually add the remaining ⅓ cup sugar and continue beating until stiff, glossy peaks form.

7. Turn the cooled filling into the pie shell, spreading it evenly with a rubber spatula. Spoon the meringue on top, mounding it into peaks and being careful to have it meet the crust at the edges. Bake for 8 to 10 minutes, or until the meringue is lightly browned. Serve the pie slightly warm, or at room temperature.

Makes one 9-inch pie

Lemon Cake Roll

Rolled cakes, such as jelly rolls, are usually sponge cakes—or "collapsed" soufflés —baked in shallow pans and then rolled up around a filling of jelly, jam, or whipped cream. This one is filled with lemon curd, a thick custard traditionally used as a filling for tarts or a spread for toast. If the cake is served soon after it is assembled, the lemon curd will be soft and creamy. However, if the cake is refrigerated for several hours before it is to be eaten, the filling will be firmer and thicker.

Although a turn-of-the-century cookbook sug-gested the following method for saving eggs, it seems rather strange advice today: "Stir your cakes the same as usual except that you leave out the eggs. After your baking powder is added and tins greased, the very last thing before placing them in the oven, stir in one tablespoon of clear snow for each egg you would have used. Your cakes will be light and tender."

CAKE
½ cup sifted cake flour
¼ teaspoon baking powder
¼ teaspoon salt
4 eggs, separated
1 teaspoon grated lemon zest
¼ teaspoon lemon extract
¼ teaspoon cream of tartar
½ cup granulated sugar
2 tablespoons confectioners' sugar

LEMON-CURD FILLING
8 egg yolks
1 stick (4 ounces) butter
⅔ cup granulated sugar
½ cup lemon juice, preferably fresh
2 teaspoons grated lemon zest

GARNISH
2 tablespoons confectioners' sugar

1. Preheat the oven to 400°. Butter the bottom of a 15½ x 10½-inch jelly roll pan and line the bottom with waxed paper. Butter and flour the waxed paper.

2. Make the cake: In a medium bowl, stir together the cake flour, baking powder, and salt.

3. In a small bowl, beat together the 4 egg yolks, lemon zest, and lemon extract. Stir in half of the dry ingredients.

4. In a large bowl, beat the egg whites until frothy. Add the cream of tartar and continue beating until soft peaks form. Gradually add the granulated sugar and continue beating until stiff, glossy peaks form.

5. Fold one-fourth of the beaten egg whites into the egg-yolk mixture, then fold in the remaining egg whites. Sprinkle the remaining dry ingredients over the egg mixture and gently fold them in until no streaks remain. Immediately spread the batter evenly in the prepared pan. Bake for 8 to 10 minutes, or until the top of the cake springs back when touched with your finger and a toothpick inserted in the center of the cake comes out clean and dry.

6. Lay a kitchen towel on a work surface and sift the 2 tablespoons of confectioners' sugar over it. Run a knife around the edge of the pan to loosen the cake, then turn the cake out onto the towel. Carefully peel off the waxed paper, using a sharp knife to free it if it sticks.

7. If the edges of the cake are crisp or browned, carefully trim them. Starting with one short side, roll the cake and towel together into a log. Set the wrapped cake aside to cool to room temperature before filling.

8. Meanwhile, make the lemon-curd filling: In a small bowl, beat the 8 egg yolks until pale and lemon-colored; set aside.

9. In a small, heavy saucepan, melt the butter over medium heat. Add the

Lemon Cake Roll

granulated sugar, lemon juice and zest, and stir until well combined. Drizzle a little of the warm butter mixture into the beaten egg yolks, stirring constantly, then beat the egg-yolk mixture into the butter mixture. Cook, stirring constantly, until the mixture has thickened and is almost boiling, about 6 minutes; be careful not to let the mixture come to a boil.

10. Remove the pan from the heat and let the lemon curd cool slightly, then cover it with waxed paper and let it cool completely, stirring occasionally; it will thicken further as it cools. Refrigerate the lemon curd until ready to assemble the cake.

11. Assemble the cake: Gently unroll the cake; do not attempt to flatten it completely. Spread the cooled lemon curd evenly over the cake to within 1 inch of the edges. Starting with one short side, reroll the cake, finishing with the seam side down. Using two metal spatulas, transfer the cake to a serving platter. If not serving the cake immediately, cover it with plastic wrap and refrigerate.

12. If desired, for a neater presentation, trim a thin slice from each end of the cake roll to even it.

13. Just before serving, sift the confectioners' sugar over the cake.

Makes one 10-inch cake roll

Filbert Cake with Coffee Buttercream

In America, filberts, or hazelnuts, are grown mainly in the Pacific Northwest. Among the sweetest of nuts, they have long been recognized as a toothsome complement to chocolate. In this recipe, their delicious flavor blends particularly well with the coffee-flavored buttercream frosting. Be sure to use powdered instant coffee for the buttercream; instant coffee crystals may not dissolve completely.

CAKE

1 cup shelled filberts

2¾ cups sifted cake flour

2 teaspoons baking powder

¼ teaspoon salt

2 sticks (8 ounces) butter, softened to
   room temperature

1½ cups sugar

3 eggs

1 cup sour cream

1 teaspoon vanilla extract

COFFEE BUTTERCREAM

¾ cup sugar

⅓ cup water

⅛ teaspoon cream of tartar

4 egg yolks

3 sticks (12 ounces) butter, softened to
   room temperature and cut into
   1-tablespoon pieces

2 teaspoons instant coffee powder,
   preferably espresso

1 teaspoon vanilla extract

1. Make the cake: Preheat the oven to 375°. Butter the bottoms of two 8-inch round cake pans, then line them with circles of waxed paper. Butter and flour the waxed paper.

2. Place the filberts in a shallow baking pan and toast in the oven, stirring occasionally, until slightly browned, 5 to 10 minutes. Set aside to cool slightly. Reduce the oven temperature to 350°. Set aside 5 filberts for the garnish, and process the remaining filberts in a food processor just until finely ground; do not overprocess or the nuts will turn into a paste. Set aside.

3. In a medium bowl, stir together the flour, baking powder, and salt.

4. In a large bowl, cream the butter and sugar. Beat in the eggs, one at a time, beating well after each addition, then beat in the sour cream and vanilla. Gradually add the dry ingredients, beating well after each addition. Beat in the ground filberts.

5. Spread the batter evenly in the prepared pans. Rap the pans once or twice on the counter to remove any air pockets. Bake for 30 to 35 minutes, or until the cakes shrink from the sides of the pans and a toothpick inserted in the center of each cake comes out clean and dry. Let the cakes cool in the pans for 10 minutes, then turn them out onto racks to cool completely before frosting.

6. Meanwhile, make the buttercream: In a small, heavy saucepan, bring the sugar, water, and cream of tartar to a boil over medium-high heat. Reduce the heat to medium so that the mixture simmers, and cook, without stirring, until the sugar syrup registers exactly 238° on a candy thermometer, about 20 minutes.

7. In a medium bowl, beat the egg yolks until pale and lemon-colored. Slowly drizzle in the hot sugar syrup and beat constantly until cool, about 10 minutes.

8. Gradually beat in the butter, then the instant coffee and vanilla. Continue beating until the buttercream is uniform in color and just spreadable, about 3 minutes.

9. Assemble the cake: Remove the waxed paper from the layers. Set aside 1 cup of the buttercream for decoration, then spread a generous layer of buttercream over one cake layer. Top with the second layer, then spread a thin coat of buttercream over the top and sides of the cake. Refrigerate the cake for about 15 minutes to set the frosting, then spread a ¼-inch-thick layer of buttercream over the first coat. Fill a pastry bag with the reserved buttercream and pipe it decoratively on the cake. Garnish with the reserved filberts.

Makes one 8-inch layer cake

White Fruitcake

Fruitcake baking was traditionally a large-scale operation. *The Carolina Housewife*, published in 1847, included a recipe requiring twenty pounds each of butter, sugar, flour, and raisins; forty pounds of currants; twenty nutmegs; and twenty glasses each of wine and brandy. This more manageable recipe for a white fruitcake, with mostly light-colored fruit, makes six small loaves, which are perfect for holiday gifts. Bake each one in a separate foil pan, then wrap individually in festive seasonal papers.

2 cups golden raisins
1 cup chopped dried apricots
1 cup chopped mixed dried fruit
1 cup brandy
2 cups flour
2 teaspoons baking powder
1 teaspoon salt

2 sticks (8 ounces) butter
1 cup sugar
8 eggs
2 cups slivered blanched almonds
2 teaspoons grated lemon zest
2 teaspoons vanilla extract
6 tablespoons bourbon

1. In a medium bowl, combine the raisins, apricots, and dried fruit, and pour the brandy over them. Set aside to soak for at least 4 hours, or overnight.

2. Preheat the oven to 325°. Butter six 5½ x 3 x 2-inch mini loaf pans.

3. In a small bowl, stir together the flour, baking powder, and salt; set aside.

4. In a large bowl, cream the butter and sugar. Beat in the eggs, one at a time. Alternating among the three, stir in the dry ingredients, the fruit-brandy mixture, and the almonds, beating well after each addition. Blend in the lemon zest and vanilla.

5. Divide the batter evenly among the prepared pans (they will be nearly full). Rap the pans once or twice on the counter to remove any air pockets. (For easier handling, place the pans on a large baking sheet.) Bake for 45 to 50 minutes, or until the cakes shrink from the sides of the pans and a toothpick inserted in the center of each cake comes out clean and dry.

6. Let the cakes cool in the pans on racks for 30 minutes, then turn them out to cool completely.

7. Pour 1 tablespoon of bourbon over each cake and let stand for at least 4 hours. If not serving immediately, wrap each cake in a bourbon-soaked cheesecloth, then in plastic wrap, and store in a tightly closed container for up to 3 months. The cakes may also be frozen for up to 4 months.

Makes 6 mini loaves

Pineapple-Coconut Upside-Down Cake

Although fresh pineapples were sold in Eastern and Southern seaport cities in the 18th and 19th centuries, the fruit was not very popular until canned pineapple was marketed, beginning around 1910. Recipes for pineapple upside-down cake began to appear at about the same time.

1 stick (4 ounces) butter, softened to
*   room temperature*
¾ cup (packed) dark brown sugar
1¼ cups sweetened shredded coconut
1 cup sliced almonds
10 juice-packed pineapple slices, drained
*   (from a 20-ounce can)*

1½ cups flour
1 teaspoon baking powder
¼ teaspoon salt
½ cup granulated sugar
1 teaspoon vanilla extract
2 eggs, lightly beaten
½ cup sour cream

1. Preheat the oven to 350°.
2. In a small, heavy saucepan, melt 4 tablespoons of the butter over medium heat. Add the brown sugar, and cook, stirring constantly, until the sugar dissolves and the mixture is thick and bubbly, about 2 minutes.
3. Carefully (the mixture will be extremely hot) pour the sugar mixture into an ungreased 9-inch round cake pan. Sprinkle the sugar mixture with ¼ cup of the coconut and ½ cup of the almonds, then quickly arrange the pineapple slices, overlapping slightly, over the mixture, and press them down gently; set aside.
4. In a small bowl, stir together the flour, baking powder, and salt; set aside.
5. In a large bowl, cream the remaining 4 tablespoons butter with the granulated sugar. Beat in the vanilla, then the lightly beaten eggs, and continue beating until the mixture is light and fluffy.
6. Alternately add the dry ingredients, the sour cream, and the remaining 1 cup of coconut and ½ cup of almonds, beating well after each addition.
7. Spread the batter evenly over the pineapple layer. Rap the pan gently once or twice on the counter to remove any air pockets. Bake for 40 to 45 minutes, or until the cake shrinks from the sides of the pan and a toothpick inserted in the center of the cake comes out clean and dry.
8. Immediately run the tip of a knife around the edge of the pan to loosen the cake, then turn it out onto a plate. Serve the cake warm, or at room temperature.

Makes one 9-inch cake

Pineapple-Coconut Upside-Down Cake

Blackberry Jam Cake

Shelves stocked with an array of rainbow-colored preserves were once the pride of every conscientious country housewife, and jams and jellies were common ingredients in 19th-century cakes, used as flavorings, fillings, and frostings. Blackberry jam tints this cake a delicate, Victorian mauve color.

CAKE

2¼ cups flour

1 teaspoon baking soda

1 teaspoon cinnamon

½ teaspoon grated nutmeg

¼ teaspoon salt

1½ sticks (6 ounces) butter, softened to
   room temperature

1 cup sugar

3 eggs, separated

⅓ cup buttermilk or plain yogurt

1 cup blackberry jam

1 tablespoon grated orange zest

½ teaspoon orange extract

FROSTING

11 ounces cream cheese, softened to
   room temperature

1 stick (4 ounces) butter, softened to
   room temperature

2 teaspoons grated orange zest

1½ teaspoons vanilla extract

2 cups sifted confectioners' sugar

Fresh blackberries and strips of orange
   zest, for garnish (optional)

1. Make the cake: Preheat the oven to 350°. Butter two 8-inch round cake pans and line the bottoms with circles of waxed paper. Butter the waxed paper, then flour the pans.

2. In a small bowl, stir together the flour, baking soda, cinnamon, nutmeg, and salt. Set aside.

3. In a large bowl, cream the butter and sugar until light and fluffy; set aside. In a medium bowl, beat the egg yolks until pale and lemon-colored, then beat them into the butter-sugar mixture. Beat in the buttermilk, jam, orange zest and extract, then stir in the dry ingredients.

4. In a medium bowl, beat the egg whites until stiff but not dry. Gently fold one-fourth of the egg whites into the batter, then fold in the remaining egg whites.

5. Spread the batter evenly in the prepared pans. Rap the pans once or twice on the counter to remove any air pockets. Bake for 45 to 50 minutes, or until the cakes shrink from the sides of the pans and a toothpick inserted in the center of each cake comes out clean and dry. Let the cakes cool in the pans for 10 minutes, then turn them out onto racks to cool completely before and frosting.

6. Meanwhile, make the frosting: In a medium bowl, beat the cream cheese and butter until smooth. Beat in the orange zest and vanilla extract. Gradually add the confectioners' sugar, beating well until the frosting is thick and smooth.

7. Frost the cake: Remove the waxed paper from the layers. Spread a generous layer or frosting over one cake layer. Top with the second layer, then frost the top and sides of the cake. Decorate the cake with fresh blackberries and strips of orange zest, if desired.   *Makes one 8-inch layer cake*

Marble Spice Cake

Marble cakes used to be made by coloring and flavoring part of the batter with dark spices and molasses rather than chocolate. The marble swirls in this cake, however, taste of allspice and ginger as well as a delicate hint of chocolate.

SPICE CAKE BATTER

1 cup milk

1 tablespoon lemon juice

2 ounces semisweet chocolate

2 cups sifted cake flour

1 teaspoon baking soda

1 teaspoon allspice

1 teaspoon ground ginger

1 stick (4 ounces) butter, softened to
  room temperature

¾ cup (packed) dark brown sugar

4 egg yolks

⅓ cup molasses

WHITE CAKE BATTER

2½ cups sifted cake flour

2 teaspoons baking powder

1 stick (4 ounces) butter, softened to
  room temperature

¾ cup granulated sugar

¾ cup milk

1 teaspoon vanilla extract

1 cup finely chopped blanched almonds

4 egg whites

1. Preheat the oven to 350°. Generously butter and flour a 10-inch tube pan.

2. Make the spice cake batter: In a cup, stir together ¾ cup of the milk and the lemon juice; set aside.

3. In the top of a double boiler, over hot, not simmering, water, melt the chocolate in the remaining ¼ cup of milk, stirring until smooth. Set aside to cool.

4. In a medium bowl, stir together the flour, baking soda, allspice, and ginger.

5. In a large bowl, cream the butter and brown sugar until light and fluffy. Beat in the egg yolks, one at a time, then beat in the molasses and the chocolate mixture.

6. Alternating between the two, add the flour mixture and the lemon-milk mixture, beating well after each addition. Set the spice batter aside.

7. Make the white cake batter: In a medium bowl, stir together the flour and baking powder; set aside. In a large bowl, cream the butter and granulated sugar until light and fluffy. Alternating between the two, add the flour mixture and the milk, beating well after each addition. Stir in the vanilla and almonds; set aside.

8. In a large bowl, beat the egg whites until stiff peaks form. Gently fold the beaten egg whites into the white cake batter.

9. Using two ¼-cup measures, scoop a portion of each batter into the prepared pan. Alternate scoops of each batter to cover the bottom of the pan. Make a second layer of batter in the same fashion, placing dark batter on light and light on dark. Repeat until all the batter is used.

10. Rap the pan once or twice on the counter to remove any air pockets. Bake for 1 hour and 15 to 20 minutes, or until the cake shrinks from the sides of the pan and a toothpick inserted in the center of the cake comes out clean and dry. Let the cake cool in the pan for 10 minutes, then turn it out onto a cake rack to cool completely.

Makes one 10-inch tube cake

CANDIED FRUITS

Candying fruits is a time-honored way to preserve them, and the jewellike fruits make enchanting cake decorations. The recipes given here are for small, whole fruits, which can be used to create a colorful wreath. This project will reward you with a trove of candied fruits, which, if refrigerated, will keep for months. Be sure to use firm, sound fruits.

CRANBERRIES

Rinse, pick over, and drain 1 pound of cranberries; place in a heatproof bowl. In a small saucepan, bring 1½ cups of water and 2½ cups of sugar to a boil over medium heat, stirring to dissolve the sugar. Pour the boiling syrup over the berries. Place a rack over several inches of boiling water in a large saucepan. Place the bowl on the rack (the water should not touch the bottom of the bowl), cover the pan, and steam the cranberries, replenishing the water if necessary, for 45 minutes. Remove the bowl from the pan and let the cranberries cool in the syrup; do not stir them. Leave them at room temperature for several days, stirring occasionally. When the syrup is as thick as jelly, remove the cranberries and spread them out on waxed paper to dry for three days, or until they are no longer sticky. Store in an airtight container.

LADY APPLES

Wash 1 pound of lady apples. With a sharp knife, slit the skin of each apple from the stem to the blossom end. Place the apples in a heatproof bowl. In a small saucepan, bring 1½ cups of water and 2½ cups of sugar to a boil, stirring to dissolve the sugar. Pour the boiling syrup over the apples. Steam the apples as directed for cranberries (at left). Cover the bowl and let the apples cool in the syrup overnight. Transfer the apples and syrup to a saucepan. Bring the syrup slowly to a boil, then simmer, uncovered, until the syrup registers 225° on a candy thermometer. Remove the pan from the heat, cover, and let the apples cool in the syrup. Store the apples in the syrup in jars.

KUMQUATS OR LIMEQUATS

Scrub 1 pound of kumquats or limequats in warm soapy water; rinse well. In a large covered saucepan, simmer the fruits in water to cover for 45 minutes. Meanwhile, in a medium saucepan, bring 6 cups of water and 2¼ cups of sugar to a boil, stirring to dissolve the sugar. Drain the fruits and return them to the pan. Add the syrup and simmer, uncovered, until the syrup has thickened slightly and registers 223° on a candy thermometer, and the fruits are translucent. Remove the pan from the heat, cover, and let the fruits cool in the syrup. Store the kumquats or limequats in their syrup in jars, or dry them on a rack for several days, then store them in airtight containers.

The cake at right is decorated with a wreath of homemade candied cranberries, lady apples, kumquats, and limequats, in addition to storebought seckel pears. Other candied fruits—such as the cherries, angelica, and citron shown here—are widely available in specialty food shops.

Berry-Orange Ice Cream Cake

Virtually any fruit-flavored ice cream, store-bought or homemade, can be used as a filling for this cake. Or, start with a pint of vanilla and stir in fresh or frozen blueberries, raspberries, blackberries, pitted sweet cherries, peaches, or nectarines (cut up or dice the larger berries and fruits). Just before serving, decorate the cake with fresh whole berries or slices of fruit.

A 1916 book of household hints suggested the following "Improvised Cake-mixer" as a time- and labor-saving device: "By putting the ingredients into a two-quart ice cream freezer you can beat them quickly and easily, the result being cakes of very fine grain. The eggs should be whipped before being added, for the best results, and the other ingredients put together in the usual order."

1⅓ cups sifted cake flour
¾ teaspoon baking powder
¼ teaspoon salt
5 eggs, separated
1¼ cups granulated sugar
3 tablespoons milk
2 teaspoons grated orange zest

¼ teaspoon orange extract
½ teaspoon cream of tartar
1 pint strawberry ice cream
½ pint heavy cream
¼ cup sifted confectioners' sugar
Fresh strawberries, for garnish

1. Make the cake: Preheat the oven to 350°. Butter a 13 x 9-inch cake pan and line the bottom with waxed paper. Butter the waxed paper, then flour the pan.

2. In a small bowl, stir together the flour, baking powder, and salt.

3. In a large bowl, beat the egg yolk and granulated sugar until the mixture is pale and lemon-colored. Add the milk, then beat in the orange zest and extract.

4. Gradually beat in the flour mixture, beating well after each addition.

5. In another large bowl, beat the egg whites until frothy. Add the cream of tartar and continue beating until stiff peaks form. Fold one-fourth of the beaten egg whites into the batter, then fold in the remaining egg whites.

6. Spread the batter evenly in the prepared pan. Rap the pan once or twice on the counter to remove any air pockets. Bake for 25 to 30 minutes, or until the cake shrinks from the sides of the pan and a toothpick inserted in the center of the cake comes out clean and dry. Let the cake cool in the pan for 10 minutes, then turn it out onto a rack to cool completely before assembling.

7. Set out the ice cream to soften at room temperature until just spreadable. Meanwhile, remove the waxed paper from the cake. Cut the cake in half lengthwise to form two 13 x 4½-inch layers. Place one layer of cake on a large sheet of foil.

8. Spread the ice cream over the bottom layer, then cover it with the second layer, pressing it down lightly. Wrap the cake in the foil and place it in the freezer until the ice cream is firm, at least 3 hours, or overnight.

9. Just before serving, trim the sides of the cake with a long, serrated knife to create a smooth surface. Transfer the cake to a serving platter. In a large bowl, whip the cream until soft peaks form. Gradually add the confectioners' sugar and continue whipping until the cream holds stiff peaks.

10. Reserve ¾ cup of whipped cream for decorating, then spread a thick layer of whipped cream over the top and sides of the cake. Pipe the reserved whipped cream decoratively around the edges of the cake, and garnish with whole strawberries. If not serving immediately, return the cake to the freezer. *Makes one 13-inch loaf cake*

Berry-Orange Ice Cream Cake

Poppyseed Cake

Poppyseed Cake

Basically a pound cake, this recipe contains a generous half-cup of poppy seeds, which add a toasty flavor and a delightful crunch. Seed cake—traditionally made with caraway seed—was a beloved Victorian dessert. Irma Rombauer, author of *Joy of Cooking*, wrote that seed cake reminded her of "antimacassars and aspidistras."

CAKE
3 cups flour
1½ teaspoons baking powder
½ teaspoon salt
3 sticks (12 ounces) butter, softened to
    room temperature
1½ cups granulated sugar
5 eggs

2 teaspoons vanilla extract
½ cup poppy seeds
1 cup sour cream

GLAZE
⅔ cup sifted confectioners' sugar
About 1 tablespoon lemon juice

    1. Make the cake: Preheat the oven to 350°. Butter and flour a Bundt pan or 10-inch tube pan.
    2. In a medium bowl, stir together the flour, baking powder, and salt; set aside.
    3. In a large bowl, cream the butter and granulated sugar until light and fluffy. Beat in the eggs, one at a time, beating well after each addition; then beat in the vanilla.

Beat in the poppy seeds. Alternating between the two, gradually add the dry ingredients and the sour cream, beating well after each addition.

4. Spread the batter evenly in the prepared pan. Rap the pan once or twice on the counter to remove any air pockets. Bake for 50 to 55 minutes, or until the top of the cake springs back when touched, and a toothpick inserted in the center of the cake comes out clean and dry.

5. Let the cake cool in the pan on a rack for 10 minutes, then turn it out onto the rack to cool completely.

6. Meanwhile, make the glaze: In a small bowl, stir together the confectioners' sugar and 1 tablespoon of lemon juice until smooth. Add up to 1 teaspoon more lemon juice, if necessary, to make it pourable. Place the cake on a serving dish, rounded-side up, and drizzle the glaze over the top.   *Makes one 10-inch tube cake*

Apple Cake

When the apple harvest begins, try his homey cake, full of apples, nuts, and raisins. Cinnamon and nutmeg give it a spicy flavor and aroma that are especially welcome in the fall. A square of apple cake is a treat at breakfast or brunch; it's also a comforting dessert, especially topped with a scoop of rum-raisin ice cream.

3 medium Granny Smith or other tart green apples (about 1½ pounds)	*½ teaspoon salt*
¼ cup lemon juice	*1 stick (4 ounces) butter, softened to room temperature*
1 teaspoon grated lemon zest	*⅔ cup (packed) dark brown sugar*
1½ cups flour	*2 eggs, lightly beaten*
1 teaspoon baking soda	*1 cup raisins*
1 teaspoon cinnamon	*1 cup coarsely chopped walnuts*
½ teaspoon grated nutmeg	*1 teaspoon vanillla extract*

1. Preheat the oven to 350°. Butter and flour a 9-inch square baking pan.

2. Peel and finely chop or grate the apples. Place the apples in a bowl, add the lemon juice and zest, and toss well to coat the apples; set aside.

3. In a small bowl, stir together the flour, baking soda, cinnamon, nutmeg, and salt; set aside.

4. In a medium bowl, cream the butter and sugar. Beat in the eggs.

5. Gradually add the dry ingredients, beating well after each addition. Add the apple mixture, the raisins, walnuts, and vanilla, and stir until well blended.

6. Spread the batter evenly in the prepared pan, smoothing the top with a rubber spatula. Rap the pan once or twice on the counter to remove any air pockets. Bake for 45 to 50 minutes, or until the cake shrinks from the sides of the pan and a toothpick inserted in the center of the cake comes out clean and dry.

7. Let the cake cool in the pan on a rack, then cut it into squares and serve it directly from the pan.   *Makes one 9-inch square cake*

The following tip for keeping loaf cakes fresh was contributed by a subscriber to the National Magazine, *and was published in* Little Helps for Home-Makers *in 1909: "I generally cut a loaf of cake in the middle and take as many slices as needed, then bring the two cut surfaces together again, [so] the cake has no cut surface exposed to the air to dry."*

THE PILLSBURY BAKE-OFF

For generations, American cooks have brought their family favorites to country fairs—or prepared them in "cook-offs"—in hopes of a blue ribbon. By far the most famous of these competitions is the Pillsbury Bake-Off, begun in 1949 as the "Grand National Recipe Hunt and Baking Contest," and still flourishing today.

The basic structure of the contest has not changed: from thousands of recipes sent in by home cooks, Pillsbury selects 100 finalists to compete for cash prizes of up to $40,000. In 1949, the only ingredient requirement was that each recipe include a half cup of Pillsbury's flour; since then, categories have been created for other Pillsbury products.

In the contest's first decade, most entrants were full-time housewives, many of whom entered fancifully named "scratch" cakes like Orange Kiss-Me Cake and Blueberry Boy-Bait. But the 1951 Bake-Off saw the first male prizewinner; his entry was Hot Ziggities, a main-dish variation on "pigs in blankets." Few recipes from that era required unusual ingredients, but in 1954, a winner called Open Sesame Pie caused a run on the then-exotic sesame seed, which has been a supermarket staple ever since.

The increasing use of packaged foods in the American household was clearly shown in the Bake-Off recipes of the 1960s. Two entries from that decade were Pantry Stroganoff (made with canned white sauce, French fried onions, and Vienna sausage) and Easy Livin' Caramel Cake (made with potato flakes and frosting mix).

In 1970, the nation's growing health consciousness was reflected in the number of recipes using molasses, whole grains, and wheat germ. Entries included Bran-New Peanut Cookies and Corn Chip Molasses Bread. A main dish, Souper Beef Supper, was awarded a special nutrition prize.

In 1988, each Bake-Off recipe was placed in one of four new divisions: Quick Ideas; Wholesome Alternatives; Ethnic Specialties; or Indulgent Treats. Not surprisingly, these categories summed up the contemporary American appetite—including an undying passion for sweets. Trendy recipes from the late 1980s included Easy Vegetable Bulgur Salad and Chocolate Praline Layer Cake.

Here's Hoping!....

Microwave

Pillsbury's 15th BAKE-OFF

BAKE

Pillsbury's BEST XXXX

63

Raspberry Cheesecake

Although it has become an American restaurant mainstay, cheesecake originated in Europe. Martha Washington's recipe, recorded in the handwritten family cookbook she inherited, called for "new milk" and rennet (added to turn the milk into cheese), butter, cream, sugar, currants, rosewater, and nutmeg.

1 package (8½ ounces) chocolate wafers
⅓ cup butter, melted
2 packages (8 ounces each) cream cheese,
*   softened to room temperature*
¾ cup sugar
1 tablespoon flour

1 cup sour cream
3 eggs
3 tablespoons lemon juice, preferably fresh
2 teaspoons vanilla extract
¼ cup seedless raspberry jam
½ pint fresh raspberries

1. Preheat the oven to 350°.
2. Make the crust: In a food processor or blender, process the chocolate wafers to fine crumbs; transfer the crumbs to a bowl. Add the melted butter and stir to combine, then pat the crumb mixture into the bottom and halfway up the sides of an 8½-inch springform pan; set aside.
3. Make the filling: In a medium bowl, beat the cream cheese and sugar until smooth. Beat in the flour, then the sour cream. Beat in the eggs, one at a time, beating well after each addition.
4. Add the lemon juice and vanilla, and beat until smooth. Pour the filling into the crust (the filling will rise above the crust). Bake for 1 hour to 1 hour and 10 minutes, or until the filling is set. Let the cake cool completely in the pan on a rack.
5. To serve, place the pan on a serving platter and remove the rim of the pan. Warm the jam in a small saucepan over low heat just until it is pourable. Arrange the raspberries decoratively on top of the cake and spoon the jam over them.

Makes one 8½-inch cake

COOKIE
MOLDS

Simple or elaborate works of edible art, cookies made with molds are a centuries-old Northern European specialty brought to this country in the 17th and 18th centuries and long since adopted—and adapted—by American cooks.

The most common type of molded cookie is one made with a dough stiff enough to retain the mold's image. From the British Isles come recipes for spicy gingerbread and rich Scottish shortbread; from Germany come such holiday treats as *springerle* (hard anise-flavored cookies) and *lebkuchen* (honey cakes); and from other parts of Northern Europe come gingerbread-like cookies such as Swiss *tirggel* and *leckerli*, and Dutch *speculaas*.

Cookie molds—both antique and modern—come in a variety of forms. Individual wood, glass, or ceramic stamps are used to press designs into one cookie at a time. Carved wooden or cast-metal rolling pins, and wooden "cake prints," can mass-produce sheets of embossed dough. There are also shaped molds, usually ceramic, in which the dough is actually baked, giving the cookies a distinctive silhouette as well as a raised design.

Among the cookie molds at right are an antique cast-metal rolling pin (middle, right), a modern cast-iron cookie pan (top, right), and two wooden shortbread molds: a modern one with a thistle design (top, center) and an antique mold (bottom, center) with the words "The World's Delicious Shortbread" carved in the bottom.

Chocolate-Drizzled Toffee Bars

Chocolate-Drizzled Toffee Bars

A buttery crust, toasted-almond topping, and chocolate glaze give these cookies a sophisticated richness. Serve them for tea, or as an elegant dessert with demitasse.

CRUST
2 sticks (8 ounces) butter, softened to
room temperature
1 cup granulated sugar
1 egg
2 cups flour

NUT TOPPING
1 cup whole unblanched almonds

4 tablespoons butter, softened to room
temperature
⅔ cup (packed) dark brown sugar
1 teaspoon vanilla extract

CHOCOLATE GLAZE
2 ounces semisweet chocolate
1 tablespoon vegetable shortening
½ teaspoon vanilla extract

1. Preheat the oven to 300°. Grease and flour an 11 x 7-inch baking pan.

2. Make the crust: In a medium bowl, cream the butter and granulated sugar. Beat in the egg, then add the flour and mix until blended. Spread the dough evenly in the bottom of the prepared pan and bake for 20 minutes. Set the crust aside to cool slightly and increase the oven temperature to 350°.

3. Meanwhile, make the nut topping: Place the almonds in an ungreased, heavy skillet and toast them over medium-high heat, shaking the pan frequently, until golden brown, 5 to 10 minutes. Briefly cool, then coarsely chop the almonds.

4. In a small saucepan, combine the butter and brown sugar. Cook over medium heat, stirring frequently, until the butter melts and the sugar dissolves. Remove the pan from the heat and stir in the vanilla.

5. Spread the sugar mixture evenly over the crust. Sprinkle the chopped almonds on top and bake for another 20 minutes, or until the topping is set.

6. Meanwhile, make the chocolate glaze: In the top of a double boiler over hot, not simmering, water, melt the chocolate and vegetable shortening and stir until smooth. Stir in the vanilla.

7. Drizzle the chocolate glaze over the nut topping. Let cool in the pan on a rack, then cut into 20 bars.

Makes 20

Toasted Almond Brownies

Though cakelike in texture, these brownies are undeniably rich—a half pound of chocolate guarantees an intense flavor. For a crunchy texture, crisp pan-toasted almonds are added instead of the more commonly used walnuts or pecans.

½ cup chopped almonds
4 ounces semisweet chocolate
4 ounces unsweetened chocolate
1 cup flour
1 teaspoon baking powder
¼ teaspoon salt

2 sticks (8 ounces) butter, softened to
  room temperature
1⅔ cups sugar
3 eggs
1 teaspoon vanilla extract

1. Preheat the oven to 350°. Grease and flour an 11 x 7-inch baking pan.

2. Toast the almonds in a small, heavy skillet over medium-high heat, shaking the pan frequently, until golden brown, 5 to 10 minutes; set aside to cool slightly.

3. Meanwhile, cut the semisweet and unsweetened chocolate into large pieces. In the top of a double boiler over hot, not simmering, water, melt the chocolate, stirring until smooth. Set aside to cool slightly.

4. In a small bowl, stir together the flour, baking powder, and salt.

5. In a large bowl, cream the butter and sugar until light and fluffy. Beat in the eggs, one at a time, beating well after each addition. Beat in the vanilla. Add the melted chocolate and mix until well blended, then gradually add the dry ingredients, beating well after each addition. Stir in the almonds.

6. Spread the batter evenly in the prepared pan. Rap the pan once or twice on the counter to remove any air pockets. Bake for 45 to 50 minutes, or until the brownies shrink from the sides of the pan, and a toothpick inserted in the center comes out clean and dry.

7. Let cool in the pan on a rack, then cut into 20 bars.

Makes 20

The term "brownie" has not always been applied to a fudgy bar cookie. Some 19th-century brownies (including Fannie Farmer's) were made with chopped nuts, but no chocolate; others were drop cookies; and some bar cookies resembling modern-day brownies were called "Indians." But by 1906, a published recipe similar to the brownies we know and love today concluded: "These 'Brownies' are a pleasing addition . . . when serving refreshments and will keep some time, if you hide them."

Hermits

These mysterious-sounding New England cookies—named, perhaps, in tribute to their good keeping qualities—are a favorite in lunchboxes and picnic baskets.

2 cups flour

1 teaspoon cinnamon

½ teaspoon allspice

½ teaspoon nutmeg

½ teaspoon baking powder

¼ teaspoon salt

1 stick (4 ounces) butter, softened to
    room temperature

¾ cup (packed) dark brown sugar

2 eggs

¼ cup molasses

1 teaspoon vanilla extract

1 cup golden raisins

1 cup coarsely chopped walnuts

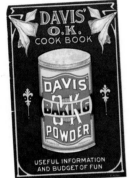

1. Preheat the oven to 350°. Lightly grease a baking sheet.

2. In a small bowl, stir together the flour, cinnamon, allspice, nutmeg, baking powder, and salt.

3. In a large bowl, cream the butter and sugar until light and fluffy. Beat in the eggs, one at a time, beating well after each addition. Beat in the molasses and the vanilla. Gradually add the dry ingredients, beating well after each addition until the dough is smooth. Stir in the raisins and walnuts.

4. Drop the cookie dough by the tablespoon onto the prepared baking sheet, leaving 2 inches of space between them. Bake for 15 to 17 minutes, or until the cookies are lightly browned on the edges.

5. Cool the cookies on a rack.

Makes about 4 dozen

Apricot-Nut Bars

Part of the mixture used for the bottom crust is sprinkled on top of these bars, like a crunchy walnut streusel. The filling is made of dried apricots cooked with apple juice and brown sugar.

1½ cups dried apricots

½ cup apple juice

¼ cup (packed) light brown sugar

1½ cups flour

½ teaspoon baking soda

¼ teaspoon salt

1 stick (4 ounces) chilled butter, cut into pieces

1 cup chopped walnuts

⅓ cup granulated sugar

2 teaspoons grated orange zest

1. Preheat the oven to 350°. Grease and flour an 8-inch square baking pan.

2. In a small saucepan, combine the apricots, apple juice, and brown sugar, and bring to a boil over medium heat. Cover the pan, reduce the heat to medium-low, and simmer the mixture until the apricots are tender, about 10 minutes. Remove the pan from the heat and set aside, uncovered, to cool slightly.

3. Transfer the apricot mixture to a food processor or blender and process, pulsing the machine on and off, until the mixture is a spreadable consistency, 5 to 10 seconds. Set the filling aside.

4. Make the crust: In a medium bowl, stir together the flour, baking soda, and salt. Using a pastry blender or two knives, cut in the butter until the mixture resembles cornmeal. Stir in the walnuts, sugar, and orange zest; the mixture will be crumbly.

5. Set aside ⅔ cup of the crust mixture for the topping, then pat the remaining mixture evenly over the bottom of the prepared baking pan. Bake the crust for 10 minutes, or until firm.

6. Carefully spread the apricot filling over the crust, then sprinkle the reserved crust mixture evenly over the filling. Bake for another 25 to 30 minutes, or until the topping is golden.

7. Let cool in the pan on a rack, then cut into 20 bars. *Makes 20*

Snickerdoodles

Although the word sounds as if it might have German origins, "snickerdoodle" is probably just another pleasingly nonsensical cookie name, like "Joe Froggers" and "Lizzies." Comfortingly homey, with warm spices, walnuts, and raisins, these tasty treats might also be called "sugar, spice, and everything nice" cookies.

2½ cups flour
1 teaspoon baking soda
1 teaspoon cream of tartar
2 teaspoons cinnamon
½ teaspoon nutmeg
¼ teaspoon salt
*2 sticks (8 ounces) butter, softened to
    room temperature*

1½ cups sugar
2 eggs
1 teaspoon vanilla extract
1 cup raisins
1 cup coarsely chopped walnuts

1. Preheat the oven to 375°. Lightly grease a baking sheet.

2. In a small bowl, stir together the flour, baking soda, cream of tartar, 1 teaspoon of the cinnamon, the nutmeg, and salt.

3. In a large bowl, cream the butter and 1¼ cups of the sugar until light and fluffy. Beat in the eggs, one at a time, beating well after each addition. Beat in the vanilla. Gradually add the dry ingredients, beating well after each addition. Stir in the raisins and walnuts.

4. In a shallow bowl, stir together the remaining ¼ cup sugar and 1 teaspoon cinnamon. Shape the dough into 1-inch balls, then roll them in the cinnamon sugar. Place the balls on the prepared baking sheet, leaving 2 inches of space between them. Bake for 12 to 15 minutes, or until the cookies have spread and are lightly browned around the edges.

5. Cool the cookies on a rack. *Makes 5 to 6 dozen*

Twist the top of th[e]
would a pastry bag
into the point. Mak[e]
for each color of ic[ing]

COOKIE JARS

The ancestors of the delightful cookie jars that brighten our kitchens were the stoneware crocks used for centuries in American homes. Cookies were stored in "stone jars" to preserve their freshness.

In the 1920s, inspired perhaps by the china "biscuit jars" of Victorian England, American art potteries began to produce hand-painted cookie jars in limited editions. By the 1930s, however, colorful mass-produced jars, durably glazed for everyday use, were staples of firms such as Ohio's McCoy Pottery Company.

Today, collectors of old cookie jars can find plentiful "pickings" at antique shows, flea markets, and tag sales. Although the early limited editions are eagerly sought by some, it is the playful jars from the 1940s through the 1960s, still relatively inexpensive, that seem to attract the majority of cookie-jar lovers.

Keep an eye on condition when buying a cookie jar, as cracks and chips will lessen its value. Also, beware of reproductions. Although some old jars bear maker's marks, many do not. One way to distinguish an old piece is by its weight: new imports are lighter than old American jars. Finally, check the fit and color match to determine whether the bottom and top belong together. "Married" cookie jars are less desirable than those that were "made for each other."

For a collecting challenge, seek out all the variations of one model, such as the McCoy apple-topped basket (bottom left), which was also made with pear, banana, pine-cone, and puppy lids.

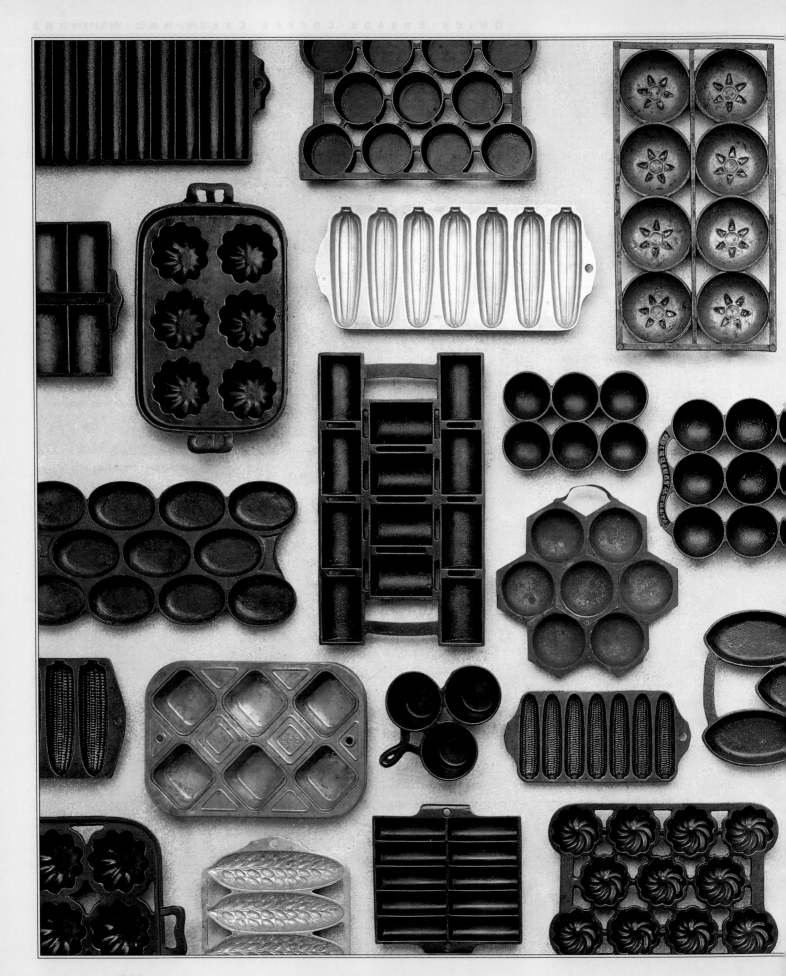

MUFFIN PANS

Before the middle of the 19th century, cooks used patty pans (small pie tins), stoneware cups, or individual metal molds for baking diminutive breads, rolls, cakes, and biscuits. One of the first multi-unit joined pans, forerunner of today's muffin tins, was patented in 1859.

By the late 1800s, American cookbooks included recipes for "gems" —small muffins and rolls—which were to be baked in "gem pans," very much like modern muffin pans. In 1893, *Miss Parloa's Young Housekeeper* included "muffin pans, two—each holding eight or twelve muffins" in a list of kitchen "articles most in use."

The earliest joined muffin pans were sets of small cups connected with a heavy wire or a soldered strip of tin. These "cut and pieced" pans were succeeded by those made of stamped tin; cast-iron and tinned-iron pans came later. Griswold, a cookware company located in Erie, Pennsylvania, was one of the first American producers of cast-iron pans; today, Griswold products remain popular with kitchenware collectors. Surprisingly, cast-iron cornstick pans (which turn out breads shaped like ears of corn) are a relatively recent invention; although they may have existed by 1900, they were not patented until 1920.

In the collection displayed here, antique and contemporary pans of iron, tin, and aluminum show a remarkable variety of pattern and form. With proper care, old pans can be used to turn out muffins and cornsticks that recall an earlier era.

Blueberry Muffins with Almonds

Every expert country cook needs a good blueberry muffin recipe, and since muffin-making is quite simple, this one might also be a good starting point for teaching children to bake. In summer, the lesson could begin with a trip to a pick-your-own berry farm—an inspiring start for young bakers. Bring home some extra berries to freeze, or bake an extra batch of muffins and freeze them for winter mornings.

2 cups flour	1 cup milk
½ cup plus 1 tablespoon sugar	4 tablespoons butter, melted
2 teaspoons baking powder	1 cup blueberries
½ teaspoon baking soda	½ cup coarsely chopped almonds
¼ teaspoon salt	2 teaspoons grated orange zest
1 egg, lightly beaten	

1. Preheat the oven to 425°. Butter and flour 12 muffin tin cups, or line them with paper baking cups.

2. In a large bowl, stir together the flour, ½ cup of the sugar, the baking powder, baking soda, and salt, and make a well in the center.

3. In a small bowl, stir together the egg, milk, and butter. Pour the egg mixture into the dry ingredients and stir just until blended. Add the blueberries, almonds, and orange zest, and stir just until combined; do not overmix.

4. Divide the batter evenly among the prepared muffin tin cups and sprinkle the batter lightly with the remaining 1 tablespoon sugar.

5. Bake for 18 to 20 minutes, or until the muffins are golden and cracked on top, and a toothpick inserted in the center of a muffin comes out clean and dry. Serve the muffins warm, or at room temperature. *Makes 1 dozen*

Date Nut Bread

For a proper afternoon tea, serve dainty sandwiches of date nut bread spread with cream cheese. Just be sure to let the bread cool completely so that it will be easier to cut into thin slices. If possible, cool it, then wrap it and let it "rest" overnight before slicing. The batter contains pear nectar, which ensures an unusually moist texture.

2 cups flour	1 egg
1 tablespoon baking powder	1 teaspoon vanilla extract
1 teaspoon baking soda	1 cup pear nectar
¼ teaspoon salt	1 cup chopped dates
4 tablespoons butter, softened to room temperature	1 cup coarsely chopped pecans
⅓ cup (packed) dark brown sugar	1 tablespoon grated orange zest

1. Preheat the oven to 375°. Butter and flour a 9 x 5-inch loaf pan.

2. In a small bowl, stir together the flour, baking powder, baking soda, and salt.

3. In a large bowl, cream the butter and sugar. Beat in the egg and vanilla. Add half of the dry ingredients, then, alternating between the two, add the pear nectar and the remaining dry ingredients, beating well after each addition. Stir in the dates, pecans, and orange zest.

4. Spread the batter evenly in the prepared pan. Rap the pan once or twice on the counter to remove any air pockets. Bake for 50 to 55 minutes, or until the bread is golden and shrinks from the sides of the pan, and a toothpick inserted in the center of the loaf comes out clean and dry.

5. Let the loaf cool in the pan on a rack, then turn it out to cool completely before slicing.

Makes one 9-inch loaf

Apple Cinnamon Muffins

Fresh tart apples, cinnamon, and cloves give these muffins the heart-warming taste of apple pie. Although pure maple syrup, used as the sweetener here, is expensive, blended pancake syrups, which contain little or no maple sugar, should not be substituted. "Fancy" or "Grade A" maple syrups are readily available, but the stronger flavor of "Grade B" syrup—if you can find it—will come through better in baking.

1 medium Granny Smith apple (about 6 ounces)	¼ teaspoon salt
2 cups flour	2 eggs, lightly beaten
1 tablespoon baking powder	1 cup plain yogurt
½ teaspoon baking soda	¼ cup maple syrup
1 teaspoon cinnamon	3 tablespoons butter, melted
¼ teaspoon ground cloves	¾ cup coarsely chopped walnuts
	2 tablespoons sugar

1. Preheat the oven to 425°. Butter and flour 12 muffin tin cups, or line them with paper baking cups.

2. Core and finely chop the unpeeled apple; set aside.

3. In a large bowl, stir together the flour, baking powder, baking soda, ½ teaspoon of the cinnamon, the cloves, and salt, and make a well in the center.

4. In a small bowl, stir together the eggs, yogurt, maple syrup, and butter. Pour the egg mixture into the dry ingredients and stir just until blended. Add the chopped apple and ½ cup of the walnuts, and stir just until combined; do not overmix.

5. Divide the batter evenly among the prepared muffin tin cups.

6. In a small bowl, combine the sugar with the remaining ½ teaspoon cinnamon and ¼ cup walnuts, and sprinkle the batter with this mixture. Bake for 13 to 18 minutes, or until the tops of the muffins are golden and a toothpick inserted in the center of a muffin comes out clean and dry. Serve warm.

Makes 1 dozen

COOKING WITH GAS

The expression "cooking with gas" has come to mean working quickly and efficiently, and with good reason: for the home baker, the gas stove was a revolution and a revelation. Its oven was fast-heating and easily controllable, while the piped-in fuel meant the end of wood chopping and coal toting.

Although the first gas cooking device was patented in 1805 (the first city gas company was established about ten years later), the fuel was still expensive, and many feared that the gas would flavor the food as it cooked. By the 1880s, however, gas ranges were being produced in volume and sold at popular prices.

The advantages of the gas range for baking were articulated by Betty Lyles Wilson, "America's Foremost Cake Maker," in a circa 1914 stove catalogue: "Your cake will acquire a beautiful golden brown surface and at the same time remain tender and soft. I hold this to be the particular advantage of the Acorn Range."

The biggest technological advance in gas cooking, though, came in 1915, with the introduction of the oven thermostat. The cook no longer had to gauge oven temperature with her hand, or by timing the browning of a sheet of paper. One historian wrote that for the housewife, the oven regulator "marked the real dif-

ference between the 19th and 20th centuries." A 1923 brochure for the Lorain Red Wheel heat regulator guaranteed "no anxious moments to the woman using a heat-regulated oven" and proclaimed that "cake put into an oven equipped with a heat regulator requires no watching. One can be assured that . . . it will be properly baked throughout." Another company vowed that temperature control would totally eliminate "the item of luck in baking."

In 1935, the American Gas Association boasted that "Gas cooks foods faster, better, cheaper" with the "instant heat, higher speed and exact shading of temperature only gas can give." By this time, bright enamel had replaced the black iron of the old kitchen range, and the stove had begun to evolve toward its current sleek design. In the early 1940s, as women joined the wartime job force, gas range ads promised "new freedom for women" with self-timers that could turn the oven on and off automatically. An ad from the postwar era conjured up an all-new dream kitchen equipped with a corner "baking center" and a state-of-the-art gas range. By the mid-1950s, some 30 million American households were "cooking with gas," and the energy-efficient gas range remains popular with home bakers to this day.

Green Tomato and Apple Bread

Many gardeners end up with lots of green tomatoes in the fall, when they must be picked hurriedly to save them from frost. Stored in a cool place, covered with sheets of newspaper, green tomatoes will slowly ripen. Meanwhile, there will be a stock of green tomatoes for baking (and for frying and preserving). In this recipe, a second large apple can be substituted for the green tomato, if necessary.

3 cups flour
½ cup (packed) light brown sugar
2 teaspoons baking powder
¾ teaspoon baking soda
½ teaspoon salt
1 teaspoon cinnamon
½ teaspoon ground ginger
¼ teaspoon nutmeg

2 eggs
1 stick (4 ounces) butter, melted
½ cup buttermilk, or ½ cup milk plus
*   1½ teaspoons vinegar*
1 medium apple, such as Granny Smith,
*   unpeeled, coarsely chopped*
1 medium green tomato, coarsely chopped
1 cup coarsely chopped pecans

1. Preheat the oven to 350°. Butter and flour a 9 x 5-inch loaf pan.
2. In a medium bowl, stir together the flour, sugar, baking powder, baking soda, salt, cinnamon, ginger, and nutmeg.
3. In a large bowl, beat the eggs until light and fluffy. Beat in the butter and buttermilk. Gradually add the dry ingredients, beating well after each addition. Add the chopped apple, tomato, and pecans, and stir just until combined.
4. Spread the batter evenly in the prepared pan. Rap the pan once or twice on the counter to remove any air pockets. Bake for 1 hour and 10 minutes to 1 hour and 20 minutes, or until the bread is golden-brown and shrinks from the sides of the pan, and a toothpick inserted in the center of the loaf comes out clean and dry.
5. Let the loaf cool in the pan on a rack, then turn it out to cool completely before slicing.

Makes one 9-inch loaf

*N*ext time you unwrap a stick of butter for baking, consider the complexities of buttermaking as delineated in an 18th-century cookbook: First the cows had to be "milk'd at regular and stated hours." Then, for the cream to rise properly, "the heat of the milk and its depth in the vessel" had to be carefully regulated. Finally, the milk needed to be churned at just the right speed: butter churned too quickly will be "soft and frothy"; while butter churned too slowly "loses its flavor and texture."

Cranberry Muffins

The cranberry, which is native to North America, grows wild from Newfoundland to North Carolina. However, almost all of today's commercially cultivated berries come from Massachusetts, Wisconsin, New Jersey, Washington, and Oregon.

1½ cups cranberries
1¾ cups flour
⅔ cup plus 2 tablespoons sugar
½ cup yellow cornmeal
1 tablespoon baking powder
½ teaspoon baking soda

¼ teaspoon salt
2 eggs, lightly beaten
¾ cup buttermilk, or ¾ cup milk plus
*   2¼ teaspoons vinegar*
4 tablespoons butter, melted
1 teaspoon vanilla extract

Cranberry Muffins

1. Preheat the oven to 400°. Butter and flour 6 large (3½-inch) muffin tin cups (or 16 regular-size cups), or line them with paper baking cups.

2. In a food processor or by hand, coarsely chop the cranberries.

3. In a large bowl, stir together the flour, ⅔ cup of the sugar, the cornmeal, baking powder, baking soda, and salt, and make a well in the center.

4. In a small bowl, stir together the eggs, buttermilk, butter, and vanilla. Pour the egg mixture into the dry ingredients and stir just until blended. Add the chopped cranberries and stir just until combined; do not overmix.

5. Divide the batter evenly among the prepared muffin tin cups and sprinkle the tops of the muffins with the remaining 2 tablespoons sugar. Bake for 20 to 25 minutes (check regular-size muffins after 18 minutes), or until the muffins are golden and cracked on top, and a toothpick inserted in the center of a muffin comes out clean and dry. Serve warm.

Makes 6 large or 16 regular-size muffins

Sweet Potato Swirl Bread

This colorful bread is laced with dark swirls of cocoa, a pleasant counterpoint to the sweetness of the potatoes. Whenever you have leftover sweet potatoes—perhaps after a big holiday meal—this is a delicious and novel way to use them. In cooking potatoes specifically for this recipe, you have several options. Slow baking is the method that brings out their flavor best; it seems to caramelize their natural sugar. However, if you're pressed for time, either cut the sweet potatoes into large chunks and steam them, or pierce the whole potatoes a few times with a fork and microwave them at 100% (high) power for 5 to 8 minutes.

1¾ cups flour
1 teaspoon baking soda
Pinch of salt
1 stick (4 ounces) butter, softened to
*   room temperature*
1 cup (packed) light brown sugar
2 eggs

1 teaspoon vanilla extract
1½ cups cooked, peeled, and mashed sweet
*   potatoes (about 2 medium, 2¾ pounds*
*   total)*
1 cup coarsely chopped walnuts
⅓ cup unsweetened cocoa powder

1. Preheat the oven to 350°. Butter and flour a 9 x 5-inch loaf pan.

2. In a small bowl, stir together the flour, baking soda, and salt; set aside.

3. In a medium bowl, cream the butter and sugar. Beat in the eggs one at a time, beating well after each addition, then beat in the vanilla. Stir in the sweet potatoes until thoroughly combined, then gradually add the dry ingredients, beating just until incorporated; do not overbeat. Stir in the walnuts.

4. Transfer one-third of the batter (about 1½ cups) to a small bowl, add the cocoa powder, and stir until well blended.

5. Spread the plain batter in the prepared pan, then spread the cocoa batter on top. Swirl a table knife through the batter to marbleize it. Rap the pan once or twice on the counter to remove any air pockets.

6. Bake for 1 hour to 1 hour and 10 minutes, or until the bread shrinks from the sides of the pan and a toothpick inserted in the center of the loaf comes out clean and dry.

7. Let the loaf cool in the pan on a rack, then turn it out to cool completely before slicing.

Makes one 9-inch loaf

The Carolina Housewife by a Lady of Charleston *was published in 1847. Sarah Rutledge, who compiled the book, apparently knew her potatoes, both white and sweet. "Among the various ways of dressing sweet potatoes," she wrote, "that which appears the most generally preferred, is to bake them twice . . . . This way of baking twice, makes them more candied."*

Sweet Potato Swirl Bread

Apricot-Cheese Coffee Ring

Some fortunate American bakers have inherited recipes for fruit-filled European breads—German kuchen, Austrian kugelhopf, Russian kulich, or Czechoslovakian kolacky. Here is a fine all-American version to add to such a collection, or a good starting point for one.

PASTRY

¼ cup lukewarm (105° to 115°)
    water
1 package active dry yeast
2 tablespoons sugar
¼ cup buttermilk or milk
⅓ cup milk
1 egg, lightly beaten
½ teaspoon vanilla extract
About 3½ cups flour
¼ teaspoon salt
⅓ cup chopped blanched almonds
4 tablespoons butter, softened to room
    temperature

FILLING

1 package (3 ounces) cream cheese
¼ cup cottage cheese
1 tablespoon flour
2 tablespoons sugar
1 egg yolk
1 teaspoon lemon juice
1 teaspoon grated lemon zest
16 dried apricot halves
¼ cup apricot preserves

GLAZE

1 egg yolk
1 tablespoon milk

1. Make the pastry: Place the water in a small bowl and sprinkle the yeast over it. Stir in a pinch of sugar and let the mixture stand until the yeast begins to foam, about 5 minutes.

2. Meanwhile, in a small bowl, stir together the remaining sugar, the buttermilk, milk, egg, and vanilla; set aside.

3. In a large bowl, stir together 2½ cups of flour and the salt, and make a well in the center. Pour in the yeast mixture, the milk mixture, and the almonds, and stir until the mixture forms a soft dough. Add the butter and mix until well combined.

4. Transfer the dough to a lightly floured surface and knead it until smooth and elastic, about 10 minutes, adding up to 1 cup more flour if necessary. Form the dough into a ball and place it in a large greased bowl. Cover the bowl with a slightly dampened kitchen towel, set it aside in a warm, draft-free place, and let the dough rise until it doubles in bulk, 45 minutes to 1 hour.

5. Meanwhile, make the filling: In a food processor or blender, combine the cream cheese, cottage cheese, and flour, and process until smooth. Add the sugar, egg yolk, lemon juice and zest, and process just until blended; set aside.

6. Grease and flour two baking sheets.

7. Punch the dough down, then transfer it to a lightly floured surface and knead it for 2 to 3 minutes. Divide the dough into 2 portions.

8. Roll one portion of dough into an 18-inch rope and place it on a prepared baking sheet (see Shaped Pastries, pages 132-133, for step-by-step photos). Bring the ends of the rope together to form a ring; overlap and pinch the ends together. Flatten the ring of dough to a width of about 3 inches. Using a sharp knife, make eight dia-

gonal cuts about 2 inches apart through the outside edge of the ring. The cuts should come to within about 1 inch of the inside edge.

9. Spread half the cream cheese mixture around the inner (uncut) portion of the ring, then arrange 8 apricots on top. Top the apricots with half the preserves.

10. Fold the long points of the flaps of dough around the apricot halves and tack them down with a few drops of egg yolk. Press a bit of dough from the center of the ring over each point to seal it; reserve the remaining egg yolk.

11. Shape the second portion of dough in the same fashion, then set both rings aside, uncovered, in a warm, draft-free place and let rise for 20 to 25 minutes, or until doubled in bulk.

12. Preheat the oven to 375°. For the glaze, stir the milk into the reserved egg yolk. Brush one ring with half of the glaze and bake for 15 to 20 minutes, or until golden brown. (Leave the second ring in the refrigerator until ready to bake, but no longer than 1 hour.)

13. Transfer the baked apricot ring to a rack to cool. Meanwhile, glaze and bake the second ring.

Makes two 10-inch rings

Strawberries and Cream Bread

M.T. Colbrath's *What to Get for Breakfast*, published in 1890, offered more than a hundred menus for that meal. Two included strawberry shortcake — in fact, a chapter was devoted to "dainty and delicious fruit-cake breakfasts for those who cannot relish hearty food for a summer breakfast." Here, shortcake's basic ingredients — including berries and cream — are transformed into a luscious, fragrant bread.

2 cups flour	*2 eggs*
½ cup sugar	*¼ cup heavy cream*
1 tablespoon baking powder	*4 tablespoons butter, melted*
½ teaspoon baking soda	*1 teaspoon vanilla extract*
½ teaspoon salt	*1¼ cups strawberries, mashed (about 1 cup)*

1. Preheat the oven to 350°. Butter and flour a 9 x 5-inch loaf pan.

2. In a large bowl, stir together the flour, sugar, baking powder, baking soda, and salt.

3. In a small bowl, stir together the eggs, cream, butter, and vanilla. Pour the egg mixture into the dry ingredients and mix just until blended. Add the strawberries, and stir just until combined; do not overmix.

4. Spread the batter evenly in the prepared pan. Rap the pan once or twice on the counter to remove any air pockets. Bake for 1 hour to 1 hour and 10 minutes, or until the bread is golden and shrinks from the sides of the pan, and a toothpick inserted in the center of the loaf comes out clean and dry.

5. Let the loaf cool in the pan on a rack, then turn it out to cool completely before slicing.

Makes one 9-inch loaf

SHAPED PASTRIES

JAM PINWHEELS

Here are step-by-step photographs for forming Jam Pinwheels (recipe on page 137). Complete Steps 1-5 of the recipe, then proceed with the technique shown at right. This recipe makes twenty 3-inch-square pastries; an average-sized baking sheet will hold about half of them. If you have two baking sheets, prepare both batches at once, but keep one refrigerated (for no longer than one hour) while you bake the other.

Roll out the dough to a rectangle roughly 15 x 12 inches. Use a ruler to trim the dough to the exact measurement, then cut it into twenty 3-inch squares.

Place the squares on a greased baking sheet. With a sharp knife, make diagonal cuts from the corners of each square to within ¾ inch of the center.

APRICOT-CHEESE COFFEE RING

Here are step-by-step photographs for forming the Apricot-Cheese Coffee Ring (recipe on page 130). Complete Steps 1-7 of the recipe, then proceed with the technique at right. The recipe makes two 10-inch coffee rings, which will have to be baked separately. Assemble both rings and let them rise at the same time, but refrigerate one of the rings (for no longer than 1 hour) while you bake the other.

Roll one portion of the dough into an 18-inch rope. On a greased baking sheet, form the dough into a ring and flatten to a width of about 3 inches.

Using a knife or scissors, make diagonal cuts, about 2 inches apart, around the outside edge of the ring. The cuts should come to within 1 inch of the inside edge.

APPLE-FILLED CRISSCROSS

Here are step-by-step photographs for forming the Apple-Filled Crisscross (recipe on page 134). Complete Steps 1-8 of the recipe, then proceed with the technique at right. Although a large baking sheet will hold the two loaves, they can also be baked separately. Assemble both loaves and let them rise at the same time, but refrigerate one of the loaves (for no longer than 1 hour) while you bake the other.

Spread half the apple filling in a 2-inch-wide strip down the center of one rectangle of dough, leaving a border of about ½ inch at both of the short ends.

With a sharp knife, make an equal number of diagonal cuts along both long sides of the rectangle of dough, ½ inch apart and to within ½ inch of the apple filling.

Place ½ teaspoon of jam in the center of each square. For variety, use different jam flavors and colors. Do not substitute jelly, which will melt in the heat of the oven.

Fold every other point of the cut pastry in to the right of center and tack it in place with beaten egg yolk. The points should not completely cover the jam.

Let the pastries rise until almost doubled. Brush with egg glaze and bake in a 375° oven for 15 to 20 minutes, or until golden brown. Repeat with second batch.

Spread half the cream cheese mixture on the uncut portion of the ring, then arrange eight dried apricots on top. Top the apricots with half of the preserves.

Fold the points of cut dough in toward the center of the ring, partially covering the apricots. Tack the points of dough in place with some beaten egg yolk.

Let the ring rise until doubled, then brush with egg glaze and bake in a 375° oven for 15 to 20 minutes, or until golden brown. Repeat with the second ring.

Bring the strips of dough up and over the filling in crisscross fashion. Overlap the ends of the strips slightly and pinch them together to seal.

Tuck the end pieces under and pinch together to form a small retaining wall for the filling at both ends. Set the loaf aside to rise until almost doubled.

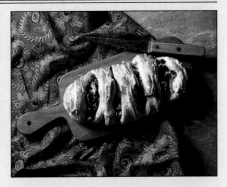

Brush the loaf with egg glaze and then bake in a 375° oven for about 15 minutes, or until golden brown. Repeat with the second loaf.

Apple-Filled Crisscross

The filling of these latticed loaves is reminiscent of apple strudel, but the rich sour-cream dough is much easier to work with than fragile, paper-thin strudel dough. For ease in shaping the loaves, the strips of dough are simply crisscrossed, not braided, over the chunky apple-raisin-walnut filling.

Northern Spy, Newtown Pippin, Sweet Bough, Black Twig, Jonathan, Twenty Ounce, Wealthy, Winesap, Roxbury Russet, Grimes Golden—the names of America's old apple varieties form a sweet poetry all their own. More and more growers around the country are devoting their efforts to preserving "antique" fruit varieties. Look for old-fashioned apples at farm markets and orchard stands; sample their varied flavors and textures, and ask about their best uses.

PASTRY
¼ cup lukewarm (105° to 115°) water
1 package active dry yeast
¼ cup granulated sugar
⅓ cup sour cream, at room temperature
2 tablespoons lukewarm (105 to 115°) milk
1 egg, lightly beaten
1 teaspoon grated lemon zest
½ teaspoon vanilla extract
About 3 cups flour
¼ teaspoon salt
6 tablespoons butter, softened to room temperature

FILLING
1 small apple, such as Granny Smith or Golden Delicious, unpeeled and coarsely chopped

¼ cup raisins
3 tablespoons coarse fresh breadcrumbs
¼ cup coarsely chopped walnuts
2 tablespoons sugar
½ teaspoon cinnamon
¼ teaspoon grated lemon zest
1 teaspoon lemon juice

EGG GLAZE
1 egg yolk
1 tablespoon milk

ICING
1 cup confectioners' sugar
2 tablespoons lemon juice

1. Make the pastry: Place the water in a small bowl and sprinkle the yeast over it. Stir in a large pinch of granulated sugar and let the mixture stand until the yeast begins to foam, about 5 minutes.

2. In a small bowl, stir together the remaining granulated sugar, the sour cream, milk, egg, lemon zest, and vanilla; set aside.

3. In a large bowl, stir together 2½ cups of flour and the salt, and make a well in the center. Pour in the yeast mixture and the milk mixture, and stir until the mixture forms a soft dough.

4. Add the butter and mix until well combined. Transfer the dough to a lightly floured surface and knead it until smooth and elastic, about 10 minutes, adding up to ½ cup more flour if necessary. Form the dough into a ball and place it in a large greased bowl. Cover the bowl with a slightly dampened kitchen towel, set it aside in a warm, draft-free place, and let the dough rise until it doubles in bulk, 45 minutes to 1 hour.

5. Meanwhile, make the filling: In a medium bowl, stir together the chopped apple, raisins, breadcrumbs, nuts, granulated sugar, cinnamon, lemon zest, and lemon juice; set aside.

6. Grease and flour two baking sheets.

7. Punch the dough down, then transfer it to a lightly floured surface and knead it for about 5 minutes.

Apple-Filled Crisscross

8. Using a lightly floured rolling pin, roll out the dough to an 18 x 8-inch rectangle, then cut it into two 9 x 8-inch rectangles. Place each rectangle of dough on a prepared baking sheet.

9. Spread half of the apple filling in a 2-inch-wide strip down the center of each piece of dough, leaving a border of about ½ inch at the top and bottom (see Shaped Pastries, pages 132-133, for step-by-step photos). Starting ½ inch from the filling, make diagonal cuts ½ inch apart, from the filling out to the edges of the dough, on both sides. Crisscross the strips over the filling. Tuck the last two strips under and press firmly to seal them.

10. Set the loaves aside, uncovered, in a warm, draft-free place and let the dough rise for 20 to 25 minutes, or until almost doubled in bulk.

11. Preheat the oven to 375°.

12. Make the egg glaze: In a small bowl, stir together the egg yolk and milk.

13. Brush one loaf with half of the egg glaze and bake for 15 to 17 minutes, or until golden brown. (Leave the second loaf in the refrigerator until ready to bake, but no longer than 1 hour.)

14. Transfer the baked loaf to a rack to cool. Meanwhile, glaze and bake the second loaf.

15. Make the icing: In a medium bowl, stir together the confectioners' sugar and lemon juice until smooth and pourable; add a few drops more lemon juice, if necessary. Drizzle the icing over both loaves while still warm.

Makes two 9-inch loaves

Cheddar-Chive Swirls

The recipe for these cheese-swirled rolls can also be used to make an impressive ring-shaped loaf: see A Savory Filled Bread on pages 146-147 for step-by-step photos.

¼ cup lukewarm (105° to 115°) water

1 package active dry yeast

1 tablespoon sugar

¾ cup plus 2 tablespoons milk

About 3 cups flour

¾ teaspoon salt

4 tablespoons butter, softened

2 cups grated Cheddar cheese
  (about 8 ounces)

2 cups chopped chives or scallion
  greens

½ teaspoon pepper

1 egg yolk

1. Place the water in a small bowl and sprinkle the yeast over it. Stir in the sugar and let stand until the yeast begins to foam, about 5 minutes.

2. In a small saucepan, heat ¾ cup of the milk to lukewarm (105° to 115°).

3. In a large bowl, stir together 2½ cups of the flour and the salt, and make a well in the center. Pour in the yeast mixture and the warm milk, and stir until the mixture forms a smooth dough. Blend in 2 tablespoons of the butter.

4. Transfer the dough to a lightly floured surface and knead it until smooth and elastic, about 10 minutes, adding up to ½ cup more flour if necessary. Form the dough into a ball and place it in a large greased bowl. Cover the bowl with a slightly dampened kitchen towel, set it aside in a warm, draft-free place, and let the dough rise until it doubles in bulk, 45 minutes to 1 hour.

5. Lightly grease 2 baking sheets.

6. Punch the dough down, then transfer it to a lightly floured surface. Divide the dough in half. Using a lightly floured rolling pin, roll each piece of dough out to a 10 x 9-inch rectangle.

7. Brush the rectangles of dough with the remaining 2 tablespoons butter. Sprinkle half the cheese, chives, and pepper over each piece of dough, leaving a ½-inch border on each side. With the rolling pin, gently press the filling into the dough.

8. Starting at one long side, tightly roll each piece of dough jelly-roll fashion, and pinch the seam to seal it. Cut each roll crosswise into 6 pieces. Place 6 rolls, seam-side down, on each of the prepared baking sheets, leaving 3 inches of space between the rolls. Using kitchen scissors, make two parallel cuts three-quarters of the way into each roll. Gently fan out the sections of each roll to expose the filling. Set aside, uncovered, in a warm, draft-free place and let rise until the dough doubles in bulk, about 25 minutes.

9. Preheat the oven to 375°. In a small bowl, beat the egg yolk with the remaining 2 tablespoons milk to make a glaze.

10. Brush one sheet of rolls with the glaze and bake for 15 to 20 minutes, or until golden brown. (Cover the second sheet of rolls loosely with plastic wrap and leave it in the refrigerator until ready to bake, but no longer than 1 hour.) Transfer the rolls to a rack to cool for at least 10 minutes. Meanwhile, glaze and bake the second sheet of rolls. Serve warm, or at room temperature. *Makes 1 dozen*

Cheddar-Chive Swirls

A Savory Filled Bread

Divide the dough into two portions and roll each portion into a 10 x 9-inch rectangle. Brush each rectangle with 1 tablespoon of softened butter.

Sprinkle each rectangle with half the filling, leaving a border of ½ inch all around. Press the filling lightly into the dough with a rolling pin.

Starting at one long side, tightly roll up each rectangle of dough jelly-roll fashion. Pinch the raw edges of dough against the roll to form a smooth seam.

Place the roll, seam side down, on a greased baking sheet and shape it into a ring. Pinch the ends together to seal. Repeat with the second roll.

With a sharp knife, make cuts 1½ inches apart all around both rings. The cuts should only go three-quarters of the way through the rings.

Gently fan the cut sections outward. Refrigerate one ring while the other rises. Brush with egg glaze and bake at 375° for about 25 minutes.

Filled breads are especially satisfying examples of the baker's art. This ring-shaped version, Onion-Cheese Ring, is rewarding for the cook and diners alike. It can be offered by itself as an appetizer, or served with soup or salad as a lunch or a light dinner.

Onion-Cheese Ring is actually a variation on Cheddar-Chive Swirls (page 144), which are individual rolls made with the same basic ingredients and shaped in a similar fashion. To prepare the Onion-Cheese Ring, use the Cheddar-Chive Swirls recipe, but make the following adjustments: Omit the pepper, and substitute 1 cup of finely chopped onion for the chives. (If possible, use red onion, as its pink tones complement the deep yellow of the Cheddar.) Follow the instructions in the Cheddar-Chive Swirls recipe through the first rising (Step 4). Punch the dough down, transfer it to a lightly floured surface, and knead it briefly. Then proceed with the method shown in the step-by-step photographs above.

Though the ring is impressive in appearance, the technique is really quite simple and adaptable. In fact, the same general recipe could be used to make a sweet filled bread to be served for breakfast, or with afternoon tea. Just substitute a sweet filling—such as raisins, chopped dried fruits, chopped nuts, brown sugar, spices, and citrus zest—for the onion-cheese mixture.

Garlic-Sage Flowerpot Breads

Use new terra-cotta pots for baking these breads. Season the pots first by brushing the insides with vegetable oil, then placing them on a baking sheet and heating in a 450° oven for one hour. Cool, wash, and dry the seasoned pots before using them.

10 tablespoons butter
4 cloves garlic, finely chopped
⅓ cup chopped fresh sage, or 1
*   tablespoon dried*
¼ cup lukewarm (105° to 115°) water
1 package active dry yeast
Pinch of sugar

1 cup plain yogurt
1 egg, lightly beaten, plus 1 egg yolk
About 3½ cups flour
¾ teaspoon salt
1 tablespoon milk
1 tablespoon grated Parmesan cheese

1. In a small skillet, melt the butter over medium heat. Add the garlic and sauté until golden, about 5 to 10 minutes. Stir in the sage; set aside.

2. Place the water in a small bowl and sprinkle the yeast over it. Stir in the sugar and let the mixture stand until the yeast begins to foam, about 5 minutes.

3. Meanwhile, in a small bowl, stir together the yogurt and the whole egg. In a large bowl, stir together 3 cups of flour and the salt, and make a well in the center. Pour in the yogurt and yeast mixtures, and stir until the mixture forms a soft dough. Blend in 2 tablespoons of the garlic-sage butter.

4. Transfer the dough to a lightly floured surface and knead it until smooth and elastic, about 10 minutes, adding up to ½ cup more flour if necessary. Form the dough into a ball and place it in a large greased bowl. Cover the bowl with a slightly dampened kitchen towel, set it aside in a warm, draft-free place, and let the dough rise until it doubles in bulk, 45 minutes to 1 hour.

5. Lightly grease 4 small (4 inches across and 3½ inches deep) or 2 medium (4¾ inches across and 4¾ inches deep) flowerpots and line the bottoms with circles of lightly greased parchment or foil.

6. Punch the dough down, then transfer it to a lightly floured surface. Knead the dough for 2 minutes, then divide it into 4 portions. Roll each portion of dough into 5 balls, then dip them in the remaining garlic-sage butter. Place 5 balls of dough in each of the prepared flowerpots (10 balls if using medium pots). Set aside, uncovered, in a warm, draft-free place to rise until doubled in bulk, 30 to 45 minutes.

7. Meanwhile, preheat the oven to 425°. In a small bowl, beat together the remaining egg yolk and the milk to make a glaze.

8. Brush the tops of the loaves with the egg glaze and sprinkle them with the Parmesan. Place the pots on a baking sheet and bake for 15 minutes, then reduce the oven temperature to 375° and bake for another 4 to 6 minutes (up to 8 minutes for medium loaves), or until the tops of the breads are golden brown. Cool the loaves in the pots for 15 minutes, then run the tip of a knife around the edge of each loaf to loosen it and transfer to a rack to cool completely.   *Makes 4 small or 2 medium loaves*

Dill Cheese Bread

This rich, eggy bread, made with cottage cheese, has been an American favorite since the 1950s, when it was baked in a deep, round dish and was known as "casserole bread" or "patio bread." This version is made as a simple three-strand braid. If possible, use fresh dill; its flavor is much more intense than that of the dried herb.

¼ cup lukewarm (105° to 115°) water
1 package active dry yeast
2 teaspoons sugar
2 tablespoons butter
½ cup minced scallions
About 3 cups flour
¾ teaspoon salt

¼ teaspoon baking soda
2 eggs
1 cup cottage cheese
¼ cup chopped fresh dill, or 1
*   tablespoon dried*
1 tablespoon milk

1. Place the water in a small bowl and sprinkle the yeast over it. Stir in 1 teaspoon of the sugar and let stand until the yeast begins to foam, about 5 minutes.

2. Meanwhile, in a small skillet, melt the butter over medium heat. Add the scallions and sauté until they are softened but not browned, about 2 minutes; set aside to cool slightly.

3. In a medium bowl, stir together 2½ cups of the flour, the salt, baking soda, and remaining 1 teaspoon sugar, and make a well in the center. In a small bowl, lightly beat one of the eggs.

4. Stir the beaten egg, sautéed scallions, yeast mixture, cottage cheese, and dill into the dry ingredients, and continue stirring until the mixture forms a smooth dough.

5. Transfer the dough to a lightly floured surface and knead it until smooth and elastic, about 10 minutes, adding up to ½ cup more flour if necessary. Form the dough into a ball and place it in a large greased bowl. Set aside, uncovered, in a warm, draft-free place, and let the dough rise until it doubles in bulk, 45 minutes to 1 hour.

6. Lightly grease a baking sheet.

7. Punch the dough down, then transfer it to a lightly floured surface. Divide the dough into 3 portions. Roll each piece of dough into a rope about 15 inches long and 1 inch in diameter. Lay the three ropes side by side on the prepared baking sheet, pinch them together at one end, and braid them. Pinch the other end of the braid together. Cover the braid with a slightly dampened kitchen towel and set aside in a warm, draft-free place to rise until doubled in bulk, 30 to 45 minutes.

8. Preheat the oven to 350°. In a small bowl, beat the remaining egg with the milk to make a glaze.

9. Brush the top of the braid with the glaze and bake for 30 to 35 minutes, or until the bread is golden brown. Cool the bread on the baking sheet for 10 minutes, then transfer it to a rack to cool completely before slicing. *Makes one 18-inch braid*

Cinnamon Raisin Bread

This irresistibly fragrant loaf has walnuts, raisins, and cinnamon mixed into the dough as well as a center swirl filled with cinnamon-sugar and raisins.

1¼ cups milk
¼ cup water
1 package active dry yeast
1 tablespoon granulated sugar
½ cup dark raisins
½ cup golden raisins

About 4 ½ cups flour
½ cup coarsely chopped walnuts
1 tablespoon cinnamon
½ teaspoon salt
4 tablespoons butter, melted
½ cup (packed) dark brown sugar

Mary Henderson, in her 1877 book, Practical Cooking and Dinner Giving, wrote, "I have remarked before that not one person in a thousand knows how to make good toast. The simplest dishes seem to be the ones oftenest spoiled. If the cook sends to the table a properly made piece of toast, one may judge that she is a scientific cook, and may entertain, at the same time, exalted hopes of her."

1. In a small saucepan, heat the milk and water until almost boiling. Pour the mixture into a large bowl and let cool to lukewarm (105° to 115°).

2. Sprinkle the yeast over the lukewarm milk mixture. Stir in the granulated sugar and let stand until the yeast begins to foam, about 5 minutes.

3. Place the dark and light raisins in a small bowl and toss to mix them. In a medium bowl, stir together 4 cups of the flour, half of the raisins, the walnuts, 1½ teaspoons of the cinnamon, and the salt.

4. Stir the flour mixture and 3 tablespoons of the butter into the yeast mixture, and beat until well blended.

5. Transfer the dough to a lightly floured surface and knead it for 1 to 2 minutes, adding up to ½ cup more flour if the dough is sticky. Let the dough rest, uncovered, for 10 minutes.

6. Knead the dough until smooth and elastic, about 10 minutes, adding more flour, if necessary, to keep the dough from sticking. Form the dough into a ball and place it in a large greased bowl. Cover the bowl with a slightly dampened kitchen towel, set it aside in a warm, draft-free place, and let the dough rise until it doubles in bulk, about 45 minutes.

7. Lightly grease two 8 x 4½-inch loaf pans. In a small bowl, mix the brown sugar with the remaining 1½ teaspoons cinnamon.

8. Punch the dough down, then transfer it to a lightly floured surface. Using a lightly floured rolling pin, roll out the dough to a 16 x 6-inch rectangle, then cut it into two 8 x 6-inch rectangles. Sprinkle each rectangle of dough with the brown sugar mixture, then with the remaining raisins. Starting at one long side, tightly roll each rectangle of dough jelly-roll fashion and pinch the seam to seal it.

9. Place the loaves, seam-side down, in the prepared pans and press gently to fit them into the corners. Set aside, uncovered, in a warm, draft-free place to rise until the dough is level with the tops of the pans, 30 to 45 minutes.

10. Preheat the oven to 350°.

11. Brush the tops of the loaves with the remaining 1 tablespoon butter and bake for 40 to 45 minutes, or until the tops of the loaves are golden brown. Let the loaves cool in the pans for 10 minutes, then transfer them to a rack to cool completely before slicing.

Makes two 8-inch loaves

Soda Crackers

The cracker barrel, proverbial centerpiece of the country general store, was the soda cracker source for several generations. But before store-bought crackers there were home-baked, which you can duplicate with this recipe. The technique of folding the dough, also used in making puff pastry, gives these crackers an especially flaky texture. The longer the dough rests, the easier it will be to handle. For the best results, mix the dough the day before you plan to bake, and refrigerate it overnight.

¼ cup lukewarm (105° to 115°) water
1 package active dry yeast
Pinch of sugar
¼ cup vegetable shortening
2 tablespoons plus 2 teaspoons hot water

About 2 cups flour
1 teaspoon salt
¼ teaspoon baking soda
¼ teaspoon cream of tartar

1. Place the lukewarm water in a small bowl and sprinkle the yeast over it. Stir in the sugar and let stand until the yeast begins to foam, about 5 minutes.

2. In another bowl, beat together the vegetable shortening and the hot water.

3. In a medium bowl, stir together 1½ cups of the flour, the salt, baking soda, and cream of tartar, and make a well in the center. Pour in the yeast mixture and the shortening mixture, and stir vigorously until smooth. Beat in up to ½ cup more flour to form a dough.

4. Transfer the dough to a lightly floured surface and knead it for about 5 minutes, adding a bit more flour, if necessary, to keep it from sticking. Form the dough into a

Honey-Graham Crackers

ball and place it in a greased bowl. Cover the bowl with plastic wrap, place it in the refrigerator, and let the dough rest for at least 6 hours.

5. Preheat the oven to 425°.

6. Lightly grease a baking sheet. Divide the dough into two portions. On a lightly floured surface, using a floured rolling pin, roll out one portion of dough to an 11 x 6-inch rectangle. With a short side of the rectangle toward you, fold it into thirds, like a letter, bringing the bottom and top over the center to make three layers. Roll out the dough again, forming a rectangle about 11 x 8 inches.

7. Using a ruler and a sharp knife, cut the dough into 16 rectangles, then prick them with a fork. Or, use a small cookie cutter to cut rounds or other shapes.

8. Transfer the crackers to the prepared baking sheet, placing them close together but not touching, and bake for 8 to 10 minutes, or until very lightly browned; watch carefully to be sure they do not brown too much. Cool the crackers on a rack. Shape and bake the second portion of dough.

Makes 32

Honey-Graham Crackers

Perennial childhood favorites, graham crackers may be made with whole-wheat flour or with the slightly coarser graham flour. Since whole-grain flours are more perishable than refined products, they should be kept in the refrigerator or freezer.

⅓ cup butter, softened to room
    temperature
¼ cup (packed) light brown sugar
1 egg
1 tablespoon milk

1 teaspoon baking soda
¼ cup honey
1½ to 2 cups whole-wheat flour
1 cup all-purpose flour
¼ teaspoon salt

1. Preheat the oven to 375°.

2. In a medium bowl, beat the butter, sugar, and egg together until smooth and creamy.

3. In a small bowl, stir together the milk and baking soda, then add them to the butter mixture. Add the honey and stir to combine. Add 1½ cups of the whole-wheat flour, the all-purpose flour, and the salt, and stir until the mixture forms a dough, adding up to ½ cup more whole-wheat flour if the dough is too sticky. Form the dough into a ball and divide it into 4 portions.

4. Liberally dust a baking sheet with whole-wheat flour. Place one portion of dough on the baking sheet and roll it out to a rectangle roughly 9 x 4½ inches, then use a ruler to trim it to the exact measurement. With a knife, score the dough, without cutting all the way through, into eight 2¼-inch squares. Prick each square with the tines of a fork, or mark it (do not cut all the way through) with a small cookie cutter.

5. Bake the crackers for 10 to 12 minutes, or until golden. Cool the crackers on the baking sheet for 2 to 3 minutes, then carefully transfer them to a rack to cool completely. Shape and bake the remaining portions of dough.

Makes 32

Sylvester Graham, born in 1794, was an American dietary reformer and temperance advocate. He believed that certain foods, such as spicy condiments, "enflamed the blood" and caused a frightening variety of ills. Graham crusaded for the use of whole-wheat flour as a purifying agent for body and soul; by the 1840s "Graham bread" had become something of a national food fad. It is the Graham cracker, however, that immortalized his name.

Sourdough Bread

This foolproof sourdough bread is made with yeast; the starter is used primarily for its flavor. The starter must be prepared at least three days in advance, but it can be kept for months in the refrigerator if you are not using it immediately.

SOURDOUGH STARTER
2½ cups flour
2½ cups lukewarm (105° to 115°) water
2 teaspoons sugar
1 package active dry yeast

BREAD
2 cups Sourdough Starter

¼ cup lukewarm (105° to 115°) water
1 package active dry yeast
2 teaspoons sugar
2 teaspoons salt
About 4½ cups flour
2 tablespoons butter, softened to room
 temperature
2 tablespoons cornmeal

1. Make the starter: At least three days before you plan to bake the bread, in a large glass jar stir together the flour, water, sugar, and yeast until well combined. Loosely cover the jar and let stand in a warm, draft-free place for 3 to 5 days, stirring once a day with a wooden spoon. If you are not using the starter as soon as it is ready, cover it tightly and refrigerate. The starter should smell pleasantly sour, and should be thick and filled with small bubbles; if it is not, the yeast is not working and you should begin again with fresh yeast.

2. Make the bread: If the starter has been refrigerated, measure out 2 cups into a large bowl and let it stand at room temperature for 2 hours.

3. Place the water in a small bowl and sprinkle the yeast over it. Let the mixture stand until the yeast dissolves, about 5 minutes.

4. Add the yeast mixture, the sugar, and salt to the room-temperature starter and stir to combine. Stir in 4½ cups of the flour and continue stirring until the mixture forms a dough, adding up to ½ cup more flour if necessary.

5. Beat in the butter. Transfer the dough to a lightly floured surface and knead until smooth and elastic, about 10 minutes. Form the dough into a ball and place it in a large greased bowl. Cover the bowl with a slightly dampened kitchen towel, set it aside in a warm, draft-free place, and let the dough rise until it doubles in bulk, about 1½ hours.

6. Sprinkle a baking sheet lightly with cornmeal. Punch the dough down, then transfer it to a lightly floured surface. Knead the dough lightly for 1 to 2 minutes. Divide the dough into two portions.

7. Shape each piece of dough into a loaf about 8 x 4 inches. Place the loaves on the prepared baking sheet and sprinkle them lightly with flour. Using kitchen scissors, make a zigzag line of deep cuts lengthwise along the top of each loaf.

8. Brush the tops of the loaves with a little water, and set aside, uncovered, to rise in a warm, draft-free place until doubled in bulk, 35 to 45 minutes.

9. Preheat the oven to 375°. Bake the bread for 30 minutes, or until the crusts are well browned and the loaves sound hollow when thumped on the bottom.

Makes two 8-inch loaves

ALASKAN SOURDOUGH

"Sourdoughs" finishing a meal along the Yukon Trail, Dyea Valley, Alaska, in 1897.

They were called "Sourdoughs"—the Alaska Gold Rush prospectors who forged northward in the 1890s. Their spartan sustenance consisted mainly of what they could gather or trap, along with bacon, beans, and sourdough breads and hotcakes.

To prepare the sourdough "starter," flour and water were combined in an open crock. Wild yeasts from the air "soured" (fermented) the mixture, which could then be used as leavening. The starter could be kept "alive" for years if it was replenished with flour and water as it was used.

Sourdough was a necessity in the Klondike because food supplies were so unpredictable. Starter provided a constant, reliable source of leavening, and it could be shared—a valuable gift. Although starter can withstand freezing, it was guarded carefully from the cold to keep it ready for use: A shelf near the stovepipe was reserved for the starter crock, but some "Sourdoughs" took the crock to bed with them to keep it warm.

To keep the starter well protected on treks out of camp, it was sometimes mixed with flour to form a ball of dough, which was then buried in a flour sack. Adept cooks could mix biscuit dough right inside the sack by kneading in more flour.

Sourdough baked goods sustained not only the prospectors, but also their pack animals and sled dogs. In addition, sourdough starter served as a soothing plaster for sprains, as a glue, and as a metal polish. The liquid from the top of the crock, allowed to ferment further, became a strong, admittedly unpalatable liquor known as "hooch."

Today, sourdough bakers prize the tradition—as well as the versatility—of this leavening process. The updated recipe for Sourdough Bread, opposite, will give you the flavor and texture associated with this authentic American bread.

Cheese Sticks

These attractive twists of rich dough are also known as cheese straws. The combination of sharp Cheddar, paprika, and cayenne give the sticks a sharp, tangy flavor, making them ideal for serving with cocktails or as an accompaniment to soups and salads.

1 cup flour
½ teaspoon paprika
½ teaspoon salt
¼ teaspoon baking soda
¼ teaspoon cream of tartar
Pinch of cayenne pepper

⅓ cup chilled butter, cut into pieces
2 tablespoons vegetable shortening
1 cup grated sharp Cheddar cheese
  (about 4 ounces)
2 tablespoons milk

1. In a large bowl, stir together the flour, paprika, salt, baking soda, cream of tartar, and cayenne. Using a pastry blender or two knives, cut in the butter and vegetable shortening until the mixture resembles coarse crumbs.

2. Stir in the cheese, then add the milk and stir just until the mixture forms a cohesive dough. Cover the bowl with plastic wrap and refrigerate for at least 1 hour.

3. Preheat the oven to 425°.

4. Lightly grease a baking sheet. Transfer the dough to a lightly floured surface. Using a lightly floured rolling pin, roll out the dough to a 12 x 4-inch rectangle. Cut twenty-four 4 x ½-inch strips. Twist each strip lengthwise, then place all of them on the prepared baking sheet. Bake for 10 to 12 minutes, or until golden around the edges. Transfer the cheese sticks to a rack to cool completely. *Makes 2 dozen*

Raisin·Walnut Pumpernickel

Unlike dense, chewy Russian pumpernickel, this bread has a relatively light texture and a sweet flavor, similar to that of Swedish limpa bread.

1½ cups lukewarm (105° to 115°) water
2 packages active dry yeast
1 tablespoon granulated sugar
2 tablespoons plus 1 teaspoon instant
  coffee
3 cups rye flour
About 2 cups all-purpose flour
1 cup raisins

1 cup chopped walnuts
¼ cup (packed) dark brown sugar
3 tablespoons molasses
3 tablespoons butter, melted
1 teaspoon salt
1 egg yolk
1 tablespoon milk

1. Place ¼ cup of the water in a large bowl and sprinkle the yeast over it. Stir in the granulated sugar and let stand until the yeast begins to foam, about 5 minutes.

2. In a small bowl, dissolve 2 tablespoons of the instant coffee in the remaining 1¼ cups water.

3. Add the dissolved coffee, the rye flour, 1½ cups of the all-purpose flour, the raisins, walnuts, brown sugar, molasses, butter, and salt to the yeast mixture, and stir to form a dough. Add up to ½ cup more all-purpose flour if the dough is too sticky. Transfer the dough to a lightly floured surface and knead it for 1 or 2 minutes, then let the dough rest, uncovered, for 10 minutes.

4. Knead the dough until smooth and elastic, about 10 minutes, then form it into a ball and transfer it to a large greased bowl. Cover the bowl with a slightly dampened kitchen towel, set it aside in a warm, draft-free place, and let the dough rise until it doubles in bulk, 45 minutes to 1 hour.

5. Lightly grease a large baking sheet. Punch the dough down, divide it in half, and shape it into two round loaves. Place the loaves several inches apart on the prepared baking sheet. Set aside, uncovered, in a warm, draft-free place to rise until doubled in bulk, about 45 minutes.

6. Preheat the oven to 375°. In a small bowl, beat the egg yolk with the milk and the remaining 1 teaspoon instant coffee to make a glaze.

7. Brush the tops of the loaves with the glaze and bake for 40 to 45 minutes, or until the loaves sound hollow when thumped on the bottom. Cool the breads on the baking sheet for 10 minutes, then transfer them to a rack to cool completely before slicing.

Makes two 8-inch loaves

Sesame Seed Biscuits

A quick hand and a light touch are prerequisites for tender biscuits. For best results, stir in the liquid just until it is incorporated, and knead the dough very briefly.

⅓ cup sesame seeds
2 cups flour
2 teaspoons baking powder
½ teaspoon baking soda

½ teaspoon salt
3 tablespoons chilled butter,
   cut into pieces
1 cup heavy cream

1. Preheat the oven to 400°. Meanwhile, place the sesame seeds in a small ungreased skillet and toast them over medium heat, shaking the pan frequently, until golden, 10 to 14 minutes. Set aside to cool slightly.

2. In a medium bowl, stir together the flour, baking powder, baking soda, salt, and toasted sesame seeds. Using a pastry blender or two knives, cut in the butter until the mixture resembles coarse crumbs.

3. Gradually add the cream, stirring with a fork just until the dough holds together. Transfer the dough to a lightly floured surface and knead it for 1 minute. Using a lightly floured rolling pin, roll the dough out to a ½-inch thickness. With a 2-inch round biscuit cutter, cut out 24 biscuits. Gather, reroll, and cut any scraps.

4. Place the biscuits on an ungreased cookie sheet and bake for 10 to 12 minutes, or until light golden. Transfer the biscuits to a rack to cool briefly. Serve warm.

Makes about 2 dozen

Pull-Apart Dinner Rolls

Hot, homemade dinner rolls may be one of life's little luxuries, but they are quite easy to make. This recipe can be baked as a panful of attractive pull-apart rolls (as shown at left), or the dough can be formed into a variety of shapes, such as cloverleafs, crescents, or buttery, multilayered fans. See Shaped Dinner Rolls, pages 160-161, for step-by-step photos.

¾ cup boiling water
⅓ cup nonfat dry milk
¼ cup lukewarm (105° to 115°) water
1 package active dry yeast
2 tablespoons sugar
About 3¼ cups flour
½ teaspoon salt

2 eggs
2 tablespoons butter, softened to
   room temperature
2 tablespoons milk
2 tablespoons sesame seeds
   or poppy seeds

1. In a small bowl, stir together the boiling water and nonfat dry milk. Set aside to cool to lukewarm (105° to 115°).

2. Place the lukewarm water in another small bowl and sprinkle the yeast over it. Stir in a pinch of the sugar and let stand until the yeast begins to foam, about 5 minutes.

3. In a large bowl, stir together 2¾ cups of the flour, the remaining sugar, and the salt, and make a well in the center. Pour in the lukewarm milk mixture, the yeast mixture, and one of the eggs, and stir until smooth.

4. Gradually beat in the butter. Continue to beat until the butter is incorporated and the mixture forms a soft dough.

5. Transfer the dough to a lightly floured surface and knead it until smooth and elastic, about 10 minutes, adding up to ½ cup more flour, if necessary, to keep the dough from sticking. Form the dough into a ball and place it in a large greased bowl. Cover the bowl with a slightly dampened kitchen towel, set it aside in a warm, draft-free place, and let the dough rise until it doubles in bulk, 45 minutes to 1 hour.

6. Lightly grease a 9-inch round cake pan. Punch the dough down, then transfer it to a lightly floured surface. Knead the dough lightly for 1 to 2 minutes. Divide the dough into 20 equal portions and roll each into a ball.

7. Starting from the center, place the balls in concentric rings around the prepared pan. Set aside, uncovered, in a warm, draft-free place to rise until almost doubled in bulk, about 30 minutes.

8. Preheat the oven to 425°. In a small bowl, beat together the remaining egg and the milk to make a glaze.

9. Brush the tops of the rolls with the egg glaze, sprinkle them with the sesame seeds, and bake for 12 to 15 minutes, or until golden on top. Let the rolls cool in the pan for 5 minutes, then run the tip of a knife around the edges of the pan to loosen the rolls, turn them out of the pan, and serve warm. *Makes 20*

Pull-Apart Dinner Rolls

SHAPED DINNER ROLLS

CLOVERLEAF ROLLS

These rolls are made with the same dough used for the Pull-Apart Dinner Rolls on page 159. After the first rising (Step 5 of the recipe), punch the dough down, knead it briefly, and follow the method described at right. For variations on these rolls, employ the same technique, but instead of three balls, use four to create a four-leaf clover, or just two large balls to make a roll resembling a Parker House.

Divide the dough into four equal portions. Roll each portion roughly into a thick rope and, with a sharp knife, cut each dough rope into nine equal pieces.

Roll each of the pieces of dough into a small ball. The balls do not have to be perfectly round; they will fill out and become smooth as they rise.

CRESCENT ROLLS

Although shaped like croissants, crescent rolls are much easier to make. Use the recipe for Pull-Apart Dinner Rolls on page 159, and after the first rising (Step 5), punch the dough down, knead briefly, and follow the method described at right. The rolls can also be transformed into breakfast pastries: make them twice as big as instructed here and sprinkle the buttered dough with cinnamon-sugar before rolling them up.

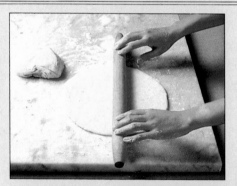

Divide the dough into two equal portions and form them into balls. Roll each ball out to a 12-inch circle. Make the circle as even and symmetrical as possible.

Brush each dough circle generously with melted butter, using at least 1 tablespoon of butter for each circle. The butter makes the rolls richer.

FAN ROLLS

These delicious buttery rolls are made by baking seven thin layers of dough together in one muffin cup. Melted butter prevents the layers from sticking together and makes the roll fun to pull apart and eat. Use the recipe for Pull-Apart Dinner Rolls on page 159, and after the first rising (Step 5), punch the dough down, turn it out onto a floured work surface, knead it briefly, and follow the technique described at right.

Halve the dough and roll it into two 12 x 10½-inch rectangles. Brush with melted butter and then cut each rectangle lengthwise into seven strips.

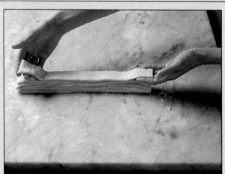

Stack the seven strips on top of one another. Take care not to let the strips stretch out as you lift them off the work surface, or the stack will not be uniform.

Roll the balls in melted butter and place three of them in each of 12 muffin cups. Set aside, uncovered, in a warm, draft-free place to rise until almost doubled.

Brush the rolls with egg glaze (1 whole egg beaten with 2 tablespoons milk) and, if desired, sprinkle the tops with sesame seeds or poppy seeds.

Bake the rolls at 425° for about 12 minutes, or until the tops are golden brown. As with all dinner rolls, these are best served warm from the oven.

With a sharp knife, cut each dough circle into quarters. Then cut each quarter into thirds to make 12 wedges per circle, for a total of 24 wedges.

Starting at the wide end, roll up each wedge and place it on a greased baking sheet. Curve the pointed ends slightly toward one another to make crescents.

Let rise, uncovered, in a warm, draft-free place until almost doubled. Brush with egg glaze and bake at 425° for about 12 minutes, or until golden brown on top.

With a sharp knife, cut each stack into 2-inch segments. If any of the layers are stuck together, gently pry them apart so the roll will fan out when baked.

Place the rolls in greased muffin cups, with the cut edges up. Set the rolls aside, uncovered, in a warm, draft-free place to rise until almost doubled.

Brush the rolls lightly with egg glaze (1 whole egg beaten with 2 tablespoons milk). Bake at 425° for about 12 minutes, or until the tops are golden brown.

Acknowledgments

Our thanks to the American Gas Association, Mary Smith Carson, Rita Entmacher Cohen, Marlene Johnson, Gene Palm, The Pillsbury Company, Joel Schiff, and Phyllis Steiss Wetherill for their help on this book. CleanTop Range courtesy of the Whirlpool Corporation.

First printing
Published simultaneously in Canada
School and library distribution by Silver Burdett Company,
Morristown, New Jersey

TIME-LIFE is a trademark of Time Incorporated U.S.A.

Production by Giga Communications, Inc.
Printed in U.S.A.

Library of Congress Cataloging-in-Publication Data

Country Baking
p.   cm. — (American country)
ISBN 0-8094-6787-9 — ISBN 0-8094-6788-7 (lib. bdg.)
1. Baking—United States.
I. Time-Life Books.   II. Series.
TX763.C68   1990   641.7'1—dc20   90-10773
CIP

American Country was created by Rebus, Inc., and published by Time-Life Books.

REBUS, INC.

Publisher: RODNEY FRIEDMAN • Editor: MARYA DALRYMPLE
Executive Editor: RACHEL D. CARLEY • Managing Editor: BRENDA SAVARD • Consulting Editor: CHARLES L. MEE, JR.
Senior Editor: SUSAN B. GOODMAN • Copy Editor: ALEXA RIPLEY BARRE
Writers: JUDITH CRESSY, ROSEMARY G. RENNICKE
Design Editors: NANCY MERNIT, CATHRYN SCHWING
Editor, The Country Letter: BONNIE J. SLOTNICK
Editorial Assistant: LEE CUTRONE

Art Director: JUDITH HENRY • Associate Art Director: SARA REYNOLDS
Designers: AMY BERNIKER, TIMOTHY JEFFS
Photographer: STEVEN MAYS • Photo Editor: SUE ISRAEL • Photo Assistant: ROB WHITCOMB

Series Consultants: BOB CAHN, HELAINE W. FENDELMAN, LINDA C. FRANKLIN, GLORIA GALE,
KATHLEEN EAGEN JOHNSON, JUNE SPRIGG, CLAIRE WHITCOMB

Staff for *Country Baking*
Editor: KATE SLATE • Senior Editor/Writer: BONNIE J. SLOTNICK
Test Kitchen Director/Food Stylist: GRACE YOUNG • Test Kitchen Associate: MARIE BAKER-LEE
Copy Editor: MARSHA LUTCH LLOYD • Contributing Editor: SANTHA CASSELL
Photographer: CHRISTOPHER LAWRENCE • Photo Stylists: SARA BARBARIS, DEE SHAPIRO
Photo Assistants: RICHARD JOHNSON, GARRY SPENCER WADE
Freelance Writer: MINDY HEIFERLING • Freelance Food Stylist: KAREN HATT

Time-Life Books Inc. is a wholly owned subsidiary of THE TIME INC. BOOK COMPANY.

President and Chief Executive Officer: KELSO F. SUTTON
President, Time Inc. Books Direct: CHRISTOPHER T. LINEN

TIME-LIFE BOOKS INC.

Editor: GEORGE CONSTABLE
Director of Design: LOUIS KLEIN • Director of Editorial Resources: PHYLLIS K. WISE
Director of Photography and Research: JOHN CONRAD WEISER

President: JOHN M. FAHEY JR.
Senior Vice Presidents: ROBERT M. DeSENA, PAUL R. STEWART, CURTIS G. VIEBRANZ, JOSEPH J. WARD
Vice Presidents: STEPHEN L. BAIR, BONITA L. BOEZEMAN, MARY P. DONOHOE, STEPHEN L. GOLDSTEIN,
JUANITA T. JAMES, ANDREW P. KAPLAN, TREVOR LUNN, SUSAN J. MARUYAMA, ROBERT H. SMITH
New Product Development: TREVOR LUNN, DONIA ANN STEELE
Supervisor of Quality Control: JAMES KING

Publisher: JOSEPH J. WARD

For information about any Time-Life book please call 1-800-621-7026, or write:
Reader Information, Time-Life Customer Service
P.O. Box C-32068, Richmond, Virginia 23261-2068

Time-Life Books Inc. offers a wide range of fine recordings, including a Rock 'n' Roll Era series.
For subscription information, call 1-800-621-7026, or write TIME-LIFE MUSIC,
P.O. Box C-32068, Richmond, Virginia 23261-2068.